Fountain of Life

A Collection of Dr. Jaerock Lee's Columns
on a Renewed Christian Life

"The teaching of the wise is a fountain of life,
to turn aside from the snares of death."

(Proverbs 13:14)

Fountain of Life

The Message of Blessings that Provides You with Eternal Life

A Collection of Dr. Jaerock Lee's Columns
on a Renewed Christian Life

Fountain of Life by Dr. Jaerock Lee
Published by Urim Books (Representative: Seongnam Vin)
73, Yeouidaebang-ro 22-gil, Dongjak-gu, Seoul, Korea
www.urimbooks.com

Unless otherwise noted, all Scripture quotations are taken from the Holy Bible, NEW AMERICAN STANDARD BIBLE, ®, Copyright © 1960, 1962, 1963, 1968, 1971, 1972, 1973, 1975, 1977, 1995 by The Lockman Foundation. Used by permission.

Copyright © 2013 by Dr. Jaerock Lee
ISBN: 978-89-7557-805-2
Translation Copyright © 2012 by Dr. Esther K. Chung. Used by permission.

First Published August 2013

Previously published into Korean in 1992 by Urim Books in Seoul, Korea

Edited by Dr. Geumsun Vin
Designed by Editorial Bureau of Urim Books
Printed by Yewon Printing Company
For more information contact: urimbook@hotmail.com

Fountain of Life is full of the treasure-like Words of God

By the sheep gate in Jerusalem there was a pool which in Hebrew was called 'Bethesda'. The water sometimes was stirred up and people thought it was angels who did it. The pool was crowded with people who had all kinds of diseases because people had been told that after the stirring up of the water whoever entered first was made well from whatever disease with which he was afflicted. A man was there who had been ill for thirty-eight years. He had suffered for a long time and because of the hope of healing he wouldn't leave the pool.

Knowing his heart, Jesus said to him, "Do you wish to get well?" and stretched His hand of love. The man replied with regret that when the water moved another had stepped in before him because he was unable to move well. Then, Jesus said to him, "Get up, pick up your pallet and walk." All of a sudden, strength came to the man and he began to walk. The man was healed of the disease that had troubled him for thirty-eight years just at Jesus' words.

Jesus was passing through Samaria and came to a city called Sychar. A woman there came to draw water. Jesus said to her, "Give Me a drink." Jesus had begun speaking to her to preach a message about the Holy Spirit which is God's gift and Himself who gives the water of eternal life. He also added that she had previously had five husbands.

She perceived Jesus to be a prophet because He knew her past life, but Jesus revealed to her that He was the Messiah. She was filled with joy because she met the Messiah and left her water-pot, and went into the city and spread the news about Jesus to whoever she met. Hearing it from her, the people in the town invited Jesus and listened to His messages, and their lives were renewed through Him.

In this way, the Words spoken by Jesus contain boundless power and the power of the creation so they solve any kind of problem in life, heal diseases, and give true life to us. That's why Proverbs 13:14 says, *"The teaching of the wise is a fountain of life, to turn aside from the snares of death."* Here, 'a fountain of life' refers to the living water that sets people free from any kind of infliction or pressure. It is the Word of God. God the Creator is omniscient and omnipotent so there is nothing impossible for Him. Everything is foreknown by Him. For us He has placed all answers to life's problems, from the beginning to the end of life, in the Bible. When we rely on God and practice His Word, we can gain eternal life and go the ways that are prosperous by receiving wisdom and understanding from above.

Fountain of Life is a collection of Christian columns that appeared on *The Gidok News.* They can be used for becoming armed with the Word of God and useful in family services. The columns cover the basic Christian information about God the Creator, Jesus Christ, salvation, the Holy Spirit, worship services, prayer, and faith. It also presents ways to become pastors or church workers who are recognized by God. Additionally, solutions to various problems like diseases and financial problems are presented in the light of God's Word.

I hope that anyone who reads this book will gain eternal life through the treasure-like messages of God and enjoy a renewed life in Jesus Christ. Moreover, I pray in the name of the Lord that in all respects you may prosper and be in good health, just as your soul prospers.

Jaerock Lee

Table of Contents

Part 1

A New Life in Jesus Christ

Part 2

Ask, Seek, and Knock

Part 3

Answers Come from God

Part 4

God the Healer

Part 5

God-pleasing Workers

Part 6

Excellent Man, Blessed Man

Part 1

A New Life in Jesus Christ

"Therefore if anyone is in Christ,
he is a new creature;
the old things passed away;
behold, new things have come."

(2 Corinthians 5:17)

God's Will Embedded in Creating Man

A skillful potter chooses good earth and makes a valuable celadon or porcelain with a lot of dedication and patience. He makes a dough-like ball of soil, creates a form, engraves it with images, puts glaze on it, and bakes it many times. In this way it becomes a beautiful and fine piece of ceramic. Another potter, however, uses the same soil but makes only earthenware with it. The value of something varies according to who made it and what kinds of materials were used to produce it.

God the Almighty created man in His own image as written in Genesis 1:27. He created man as a spiritual being who resembled not only His outward appearance but also His original heart. Revelation 4:11 reads, *"... You created all things, and because of Your will they existed, and were created."* It means that God created all things with a specific purpose and will. Then, what was His purpose in creating man?

First of all, God wanted true children.

Ecclesiastes 12:13 reads, *"The conclusion, when all has been heard, is: fear God and keep His commandments, because this applies to every person."* God wanted children who spiritually communicate with Him, revere Him, and live according to His will. However, mankind has been stained with sin and evil over time. They lost the original image due to Adam's sin. If we realize the heart as well as the body of man was created in God's image and we understand man's duty, then we ought to become His holy children by living according to His Word.

Second, He wanted to receive glory.

God is the One who is worthy of truly receiving glory. He is the One who created the heavens and the earth and all things in them, and He is the Almighty and the Light itself. There is no darkness in Him and He is holy. When we glorify Him, He does not just receive the glory, but He also gives overflowing blessing back to us and returns everlasting glory in Heaven. Isaiah 43:7 reads, *"Everyone who is called by My name, and whom I have created for My glory, whom I have formed, even whom I have made..."* Therefore, we should do everything to the glory of God—whether we eat or drink or whatever we do. We should become light and salt in the world through our good works and give glory to God as recorded in Matthew 5:16.

Third, He wanted to give and receive love.

God has a human nature as well as a divine nature, so He wants both to give and receive love. In Heaven there are countless angels that obey Him like robots. But, they have no free will so they are able to share love from the bottom of their hearts. God wanted beings that love Him and share love with Him with both the heart and free will. That's why He created men in His image. He takes care of them with great love and leads them to the heavenly kingdom.

To Become God's Children

If one's father is the king of a country, his children also have great authority. They enjoy wealth and glory in a gorgeous palace without any toil. Can you imagine how great the authority would be when we become the children of God who created the heavens and the earth and all things in them!

As recorded in Philippians 4:3, when we become God's children, our names are written in the Book of Life in Heaven. We gain the citizenship of Heaven (Philippians 3:20) and will enjoy heavenly glory forever. Of course, even on the earth we can prosper in all respects and be in good health just as our souls prosper. Then, what should we do in order to become God's children who enjoy such authority and blessing?

Foremost, we need to accept Jesus Christ.

John 1:12 reads, *"But as many as received Him, to them*

He gave the right to become children of God, even to those who believe in His name." During Jesus' ministry, Jews did not associate with either the Gentiles or the Samaritans, who were mixed-blood people. Because of this, the Jews took a detour around Samaria to avoid passing through it, though it was a shortcut to Galilee. But Jesus went into Samaria to preach the gospel to Samaritans.

While He was there Jesus came upon a Samaritan woman and asked her to draw water and give Him a drink as described in John 4:7. He knocked on the door of her mind so that she could accept Jesus. That is, anyone who accepts the Lord when He knocks on the door of his or her mind can be saved. This is the will of God.

Second, we need to believe in the name of Jesus Christ.

Jesus said in John 3:16, *"For God so loved the world, that He gave His only begotten Son, that whoever believes in Him shall not perish, but have eternal life."* Through this verse, we can realize we need faith to receive salvation. This faith is the kind of faith with which we act according to God's will and not one with which we call out "Lord, Lord" only with lips (Matthew 7:21).

When we accept Jesus Christ, God sends the Holy Spirit

into our hearts as a gift. The Holy Spirit in us teaches us the truth, brings to our remembrance what Jesus said, helps us realize we are sinners and helps us believe in the name of Jesus Christ. With His help, we can realize why God created men, what caused them to take the way of death, and why Jesus is our only Savior. As recorded in Matthew 16:16, by realizing God's will and providence, people can profess from the bottom of their hearts, "Jesus is the Christ, the Son of the living God". Such people will live according to the Word of God and enter the heavenly kingdom.

Why is Jesus our only Savior?

James Simpson made a great discovery of chloroform which is an anesthetic and relieves a great deal of patients' pain. When his student asked him what the greatest discovery was in his life, he gave an unexpected answer saying: "The greatest discovery in my life is that I was a sinner and Jesus is the One who saved me".

Just as he professed, Jesus took all mankind's sins, died on the cross, was resurrected on the third day from the death, and became the Savior. That is, Jesus is our only Savior. Why, then, is He our only Savior?

First of all, it is because He came to the earth in a form of man.

Adam, the first man, was taught only the truth by God. Naturally he had only truthful things such as goodness, love, and righteousness. But after sin entered mankind when Adam committed the sin of disobedience by eating from the tree of the knowledge of good and evil, all mankind including himself and all his descendants became sinners. So, they were put under the situation of not being able to remove the burden of sins for themselves.

They could unload the burden of sins only if a being, who was qualified as the Savior, were to pay the price of sin on behalf of them. The first qualification as the Savior who redeems us from our sins, is that the Savior must be a man because sin entered mankind by Adam who was a man (1 Corinthians 15:21). Angels and animals cannot take the burden for mankind. Therefore, in order to redeem mankind from sins on their behalf, God, who is the Word, came to the earth in a form of man. As written in John 1:14, this is Jesus.

Second, it is because He is not Adam's descendant.

Adam's descendants were all sinners who have original sin, so they lack the ability to redeem people from sins. It's just like those who are deeply in debt cannot pay the debt of other people. But Jesus was conceived in Virgin Mary's womb by the Holy Spirit in the midst of God's power (Matthew 1:20). Jesus just borrowed her womb. Since He is not Adam's descendant, He had neither inherited nor original sin, and He can redeem men from their sins.

Third, it is because He had power to redeem men from sins.

To help your brother who is on debt, you need to have money, that is, financial power. Likewise, to become a Savior for sinners, the Savior needs to have power to redeem them from sins. Power in the spiritual world is being without sin. Jesus was conceived by the Holy Spirit, so He didn't inherit any sins. He also completely kept the Law, so He didn't commit any self-committed sins. Therefore, He had power to redeem men from sins. So, the enemy devil and Satan surrendered before Jesus' spiritual authority and various kinds of diseases were healed by Him. Even the heavens and the earth and all things in them obeyed His word.

Fourth, it is because He had love.

Even if someone meets the three qualifications above, he cannot become a Savior if he doesn't have love. To redeem men from sins, the Savior had to be despised and mocked as if He were the worst of sinners even though He had no sin at all. Moreover, He had to be crucified and shed all blood (Galatians 3:13; Hebrews 9:22). How could He have endured such suffering without love? Jesus had such great love, so He could die on the cross for sinners and become the Savior. Therefore, we can receive salvation only by Jesus Christ (Acts 4:12).

The Spiritual Meanings of the Resurrection

After Adam sinned, mankind had no other choice but to go to Hell due to the wages of sins (Romans 6:23). In order to save mankind, the sinless Jesus died on their behalf. God's only begotten Son, Jesus, took the cross because of the love and mercy of God who wanted to save men—even if it meant that He had to endure terrible pain and sacrifice. Since Jesus had no sin at all, however, He was resurrected and became the first fruits of the resurrection. Thus, those who receive salvation by believing in Jesus Christ should wait for the Second Coming of the Lord and live in hope of resurrection. What is the spiritual meaning of Jesus Christ's resurrection?

Above all else it means an everlasting victory.

All men were placed under the curse of the Law that says "The wages of sin is death." It was for all mankind that Jesus received the punishment of death by crucifixion and secured the redemption of mankind from sins. Furthermore, since Jesus was sinless, He broke the authority of death, was resurrected, and achieved victory. Anyone who becomes united with the Lord in faith can be set free from the authority of death, reach salvation, and possess eternal Heaven.

Second, the resurrection symbolizes reconciliation with God.

In the Old Testament time, men were forgiven of their sins by offering up sacrifices to God with animals whenever they committed sins. But Jesus destroyed the wall of sins between God and us once for all by becoming the atoning sacrifice for our sins, redeeming us from them, and being resurrected (1 John 2:2). Therefore, Jesus Christ's resurrection means establishing reconciliation with God.

Third, it gives us hope for resurrection.

Because Jesus Christ became the first fruits of the resurrection, all people who receive salvation in Christ can also be resurrected (1 Corinthians 15:52). Due to this hope, God's children can rejoice and give thanks in any circumstance. This is like the case that if we are sure about getting a million dollars tomorrow we can rejoice today even if we don't have any food. In addition, we can work faithfully with joy and expectation for heavenly rewards and glory.

True Rest

All people have their own burden in their life. Children start to go to school at the average age of six. Some people devote their lives for more than 20 years to acquire knowledge. The end of the study doesn't mean comfort and rest. They live thinking about how they can get promoted in their workplace or how they can live prosperous lives in this competitive society. They get married, have children, and might enjoy happiness. But all of these things are accompanied by toil and pains.

There are also other burdens. Husbands should lead their family as heads of the family, wives should take care of their family members, parents should raise their children well, and children should honor and serve their parents. Also, as an employee and as a citizen of a country, all men have duties and responsibilities.

However, there is the heaviest and biggest of burdens. It

is the burden of sins. If people come to know that God the Creator is alive and that Heaven and Hell exist as real places, they realize that the burden of sins is the heaviest and biggest burden of all. Diseases and disasters are caused by sins. Sin is the cause of every kind of problem. Sins also lead people to Hell. To solve such problems, Jesus came to the earth around 2,000 years ago.

Jesus delivered His message of love saying in Matthew 11:28, *"Come to Me, all who are weary and heavy-laden, and I will give you rest."*

When you come to Jesus, accept Him as the Savior, and take the way of faith, then your problem of sins can be resolved. Jesus also said that we can have rest when we take His yoke and learn from Him (Matthew 11:29). The yoke of Jesus is to obey God's will and live according to His Word, namely, it refers to His life (Philippians 2:5-8). When we follow Jesus' example, we can become individuals who obey God's will having the heart of Christ in our hearts.

When an ox takes on a yoke and cultivates infertile ground into soft and good soil, a farmer can bear abundant fruit from the ground. Likewise, when we take Jesus' yoke and learn from Him, our heart-field becomes good soil and we can receive God's abundant blessing. Moreover, we can gain Heaven and eternal life. How painful you feel when you have argument, burst out anger, and break peace with others! But if you love everybody without hatred like Jesus did, you will be full of joy. If you want to have true rest, put down your heavy burden before Jesus Christ. By doing so, I hope you will have rest and receive blessing in the love of God who will guide you to the heavenly kingdom where there is no tear, no sorrow, and no pain.

When the Holy Spirit Comes

It is great joy to give and receive elaborately decorated gifts to and from each other even if they are just small ones. This is because they feel each other's heart in the gifts. But the more precious and valuable gift than any other gifts in the world is the Holy Spirit. The Holy Spirit is the gift God has given to us. The Holy Spirit is the heart of God, and God sends Him to us as a sign of having become God's child when we accept Jesus Christ (2 Corinthians 1:22).

After the resurrected Lord ascended into Heaven, His disciples and those who believed in the Lord gathered and prayed every day. Then one day there suddenly came from heaven a noise like a violent rushing wind, and there appeared to them tongues as of fire distributing amongst them and the tongues rested on each one of them, and they were filled with the Holy Spirit and began to speak with other tongues (Acts 2:2-4). When the Holy Spirit comes into our hearts, we gain the strength to live according to God's Word, feel His love, and boldly preach the gospel. So, what kind of roles specifically does the Holy Spirit play?

First of all, He lets us shine the light of the truth.

When we turn on an electric generator, the electricity is produced. When the electricity is transferred to a light bulb, it brightens up our rooms. Likewise, when the Holy Spirit comes into our hearts and works in us, sin and the untruth are driven away and the truth like love, joy, and thanks shine.

However, just having a generator doesn't produce the electricity and light. We need to turn it on. God gives us the Holy Spirit that plays a role of the generator, but it's up to us to let the generator do its work. The generator called "the Holy Spirit" is working when we live by the Word of God and become full of the Spirit. Then, we can brighten up things around us.

Second, He gives us strength to overcome the world.

The worldly culture is becoming increasingly stained with sin and evil day by day. If we take in the worldly things, the Holy Spirit reprimands us through the Word of God and lets us discern the truth. So, even though we once took them in, we can turn away from them by feeling His lamentation. He also gives us strength to pray so that we can do away with attachment to the world. He helps us taste joy of living in Him when we pray fervently. By doing so, He lets us love God all the more and He always comforts and encourages His children who try hard to cast off their attachment to the world.

Third, He lets us lead an abundant life.

When we live according to the Word of God by the help of the Holy Spirit, joy and peace come to our hearts and we can enjoy abundant blessings like in finance and health. As our souls prosper, everything will go well with us and we enjoy good health. Thus, we can enjoy real satisfaction both in spirit and body by the help of the Holy Spirit. Deacon Stephen manifested great signs and wonders while filled with grace and power. Nobody could stand against him because he spoke in fullness of wisdom and the Holy Spirit. In this same way, those who are full of the Spirit can manifest signs and wonders and their lives are filled with love and grace. They will continue to lead abundant lives because God's blessings overflow in them.

Secret Hidden in Regeneration

Jesus began His ministry by manifesting the first sign in which He turned water into wine. Later He healed the sick and preached the gospel of the kingdom of heaven. A number of people believed Jesus after witnessing such signs. Nicodemus was a ruler of the Jews in Jesus' time. He heard about Him and one night he quietly came to Jesus and told Him that he knew He had come from God. Nicodemus knew that no one could manifest the signs that Jesus had done unless God was with him.

In John 3:3 is the account of Jesus teaching Nicodemus that men can enter the kingdom of God only when they are born again. Nicodemus had a good heart, but he couldn't understand the message and wondered how men could be born again. Jesus explained to him about being born of water and the Spirit.

Then, what does it indicate that men are born of water?

Here "water" refers to the water of eternal life, namely, the truth and the Word of God. It also refers to Jesus who came to the earth as the Word that became flesh. John 4:14 reads, *"But whoever drinks of the water that I will give him shall never thirst; but the water that I will give him will become in him a well of water springing up to eternal life."* Therefore, being born of water is to accept Jesus Christ, receive forgiveness of sins with faith, and become born again as God's children.

Next, what does it mean that men are born of the Spirit?

After Adam, the first man, had committed sins, the spirit in all people died and they could no longer communicate with God. But when we accept Jesus Christ and receive the Holy Spirit, our dead spirit is revived. Then, our names are written in the Book of Life in Heaven and we can call God Abba Father (Galatians 4:6). Also, the Holy Spirit lets us understand what sin, righteousness, and judgment are through God's Word that is the truth so that we can cast away sins, act in righteous ways, and live as God's children.

After we sow seeds we need to take care of the crops until they bear fruit. In much the same way, we need to let spirit grow by the help of the Holy Spirit once our spirit, which was dead, is revived. We need to change our hearts into the hearts of the truth by following the desire of the Spirit and acting according to God's Word. This is the process of the Spirit giving birth to spirit. In the process, prayer is a must.

To the extent that we pray more arduously and fervently, we can receive the grace of God and the help of the Holy Spirit, and we can live according to the truth. Then to the extent that we cultivate truthful hearts, our spirits can grow and we can enter into better dwelling places in Heaven. I hope you will realize the amazing mystery in being born again and you will become born again as God's children. Moreover, I hope you will draw closer to God's throne by becoming holy men of spirit.

To Gain Eternal Life

Everyone desires to live a healthy and happy life. But, even if some people are very healthy, very few of them live for more than 100 years. And then they just return to a handful of earth. In Chinese history, Qin Shihuangdi wanted to gather elixir plants to live forever, but in the end he also had no other choice but death.

However, Jesus suggested the way to eternal life. John 6:53-55 reads, *"So Jesus said to them, 'Truly, truly, I say to you, unless you eat the flesh of the Son of Man and drink His blood, you have no life in yourselves. He who eats My flesh and drinks My blood has eternal life, and I will raise him up on the last day. For My flesh is true food, and My blood is true drink.'"* This is to say that we must eat the flesh of the Son of Man and drink His blood in order to gain eternal life.

Then, what is the flesh of the Son of Man and how can we eat it?

John 1:1 says, *"In the beginning was the Word, and the Word was with God, and the Word was God."* And John 1:14 reads, *"And the Word became flesh, and dwelt among us..."* Jesus is the Word who came to the earth in flesh. So the flesh of Jesus refers to the Word of God. Therefore, to eat the flesh of Jesus means to make the Word of God food for our hearts.

To make the Word of God our spiritual food, we need to read the Bible diligently and listen intently to the message during the service as recorded in Psalm 1:2. We cannot say that we make the Word our food when we have the Word only as knowledge. Making the Word food for us means to change our hearts by the Word of God and fill our hearts with the truthful things like goodness and love.

Next, what is the blood of the Son of Man and how can we drink it?

While we are eating food, we need something to drink. Likewise, to eat the Word of God and digest it, we need to drink the true drink which is the blood of Jesus. To drink the blood of Jesus means to practice God's Word with faith. His blood is the precious blood that is blameless and spotless. Leviticus 17:14 says, *"For as for the life of all flesh, its blood is identified with its life."* Hebrews 9:22 reads, *"...and without shedding of blood there is no forgiveness."* Therefore, Jesus shed His precious blood to redeem us from our sins.

But not everyone receives forgiveness of sins although Jesus redeemed men from sins. The reason is found in 1 John 1:7 that reads, *"But if we walk in the Light as He Himself is in the Light, we have fellowship with one another, and the blood of Jesus His Son cleanses us from all sin."* The power of Jesus' precious blood that lets us be forgiven of all sins is manifested in those who walk in the Light. Here, "the Light" refers to God's Word, so to walk in the Light means to act according to the Word. Thus, when we eat Jesus' flesh and drink His blood, namely, when we listen to God's Word intently, make it the bread of our hearts and practice it with faith, we can then possess eternal life and Heaven.

Spiritual Faith that Is Followed by Deeds

Abraham, forefather of faith dwelled in Ur of the Chaldeans. The people there worshipped idols excessively. God told Abraham to leave that place and gave him words of promise. He promised to greatly multiply his seed. And He said that in him all the families of the earth would be blessed (Genesis 12:1-3).

Because Abraham believed God, he reminded himself of God's promise seeing countless stars at night and a number of fruit of the oak. He built an altar wherever he went. When His appointed time came, God set up Abraham's grandson, Jacob, as the progenitor of Israel and laid the foundation of the nation through Jacob's twelve sons. God also sent Jesus to this earth as a descendant of Judah among the twelve tribes and opened the way of salvation to all people. Like this, true faith is *"the assurance of things hoped for, the conviction of things not seen"* (Hebrews 11:1).

There are two kinds of faith; fleshly faith and spiritual faith.

Fleshly faith is belief that things are created only out of things that already exist. With this faith, people believe scientific and logical facts like "A desk is made of wood that comes from trees." They believe God's Word only when it agrees with their thoughts and knowledge, so they don't act completely according to the Word (James 2:26).

Meanwhile, if you have spiritual faith, even if the Word is invisible and doesn't agree with your thoughts you still can believe. With God's power, the Red Sea was parted, the sun and the moon stood still, and the dead were revived. You believe such works with no doubt. Such faith is belief that things can be created out of nothing. This is living faith that is followed by deeds.

Only when we have spiritual faith can we receive blessings on the earth and enjoy eternal life and eternal blessings. Just as said in Matthew 7:21, *"Not everyone who says to Me, 'Lord, Lord,' will enter the kingdom of heaven, but he who does the will of My Father who is in heaven will enter,"* we can experience God's power and go to Heaven only with living faith that is followed by action.

Obstacles that Block Us from Gaining Spiritual Faith

Spiritual faith is the treasure of treasures. When you have such faith, you can go to Heaven and receive answers to whatever you pray for. But you cannot have spiritual faith just because you want it. You can have a measure of faith to the extent that God allots to you as written in Romans 12:3. If people were able to have spiritual faith as they pleased, they would cause many problems. If someone had spiritual faith but prayed out of evilness, evil things would be fulfilled in accordance with what he prayed for. Therefore, the God of justice allots only to properly qualified persons the spiritual faith with which they can receive answers. But what are the reasons people don't have spiritual faith even though they have believed in God for a long time?

The first is because of fleshly thoughts

People have a multitude of thoughts from moment to moment. Among them, they have spiritual thoughts that God wants, but they also have fleshly thoughts. Fleshly thoughts are all thoughts that are against the truth and they eventually lead to death because they are not in accordance with God's will (Romans 6:23).

Romans 8:6-7 reads, *"For the mind set on the flesh is death, but the mind set on the Spirit is life and peace, because the mind set on the flesh is hostile toward God."* Spiritual thoughts lead to life and peace because they follow God's will.

The second is because of works/deeds of the flesh

Works of the flesh are specific actions revealed outwardly from untruthful attributes in the heart. From comparatively small deeds like lying, foul language, and arguing; to violence and murder; works of the flesh refer to such sins revealed as actions. Galatians 5:19-21 reads, *"Now the deeds of the flesh are evident, which are: immorality, impurity, sensuality, idolatry, sorcery, enmities, strife, jealousy, outbursts of anger, disputes, dissensions, factions, envying, drunkenness, carousing, and things like these, of which I forewarn you, just as I have forewarned you, that those who practice such things will not inherit the kingdom of God."* We can possess spiritual faith when we get rid of even trivial-looking works of the flesh as well as the evident works of the flesh.

The third is because of all kinds of theories and thoughts that are contradictory to the Word of God

Because the worldly theory claims that which exists must be created out of something that existed, it hinders people from having spiritual faith that believes something can be created out of nothing. For example, having spiritual faith is to believe God brought the heavens and the earth and all things in them into existence out of nothing and believe it with no doubt. But, those who learned evolutionary theory find it difficult to have spiritual faith because of what they have learned as knowledge. Thus, in order to have spiritual faith, we should destroy speculations and every lofty thing raised up against the knowledge of God, and we should also take every thought captive to the obedience of Christ (2 Corinthians 10:5).

The Kind of the Bride the Lord Wants

In the Old Testament in chapter 2 of the book of Esther, the process used by King Ahasuerus in choosing a queen is described. Every beautiful young virgin from all the provinces of his kingdom was gathered, and it took twelve months to complete their adornment. And then, the King chose the best bride for himself.

Esther 2:12 records, *"Now when the turn of each young lady came to go in to King Ahasuerus, after the end of her twelve months under the regulations for the women—for the days of their beautification were completed as follows: six months with oil of myrrh and six months with spices and the cosmetics for women."*

The queen candidates for the king on the earth did their best to adorn themselves. Then, how much should brides of the Lord adorn themselves? The Bible likens Jesus Christ to a Bridegroom and believers are likened to His brides. So let's examine how we can meet the qualifications to be the kind of the bride the Lord wants.

First of all, we should have firm faith.

A bridegroom and his bride would most certainly be unhappy no matter how beautiful the bride might be if the bride did not believe in the bridegroom completely and was not able to share her heart with him. Likewise, when a bride of the Lord easily changes her heart and sways right and left, she can't be joy to the Lord. Only when we act according to God's Word and have unshakable faith in any situation or hardship, can we become beautiful brides that the Lord wants.

Second, we should have a pure heart.

We become a bride of the holy Lord as we wash away the filthy sins and unrighteousness that fill up our hearts with spiritual water that is the Word of God. A person who fights and gets hot-tempered should get rid of hot-temperedness and change into a man of gentleness. An arrogant person should change into a humble man who serves others. That is, we need to have beautiful and soft hearts like silk so that nobody has hard-feeling against us. Those who have pure hearts naturally make themselves and their surrounding pure and clean.

Third, we should prepare our oil by being on the alert all the time.

Here, 'oil' means prayer and fullness of the Holy Spirit. To prepare oil well is being awakened from spiritual slumber, praying, casting away sins, and becoming filled with the Spirit.

Even if we have a lamp, if we have no oil we can't brighten up the darkness. Likewise, if those who accept the Lord don't pray, they can't adorn themselves as brides of the Lord. They are not given strength to live in the Word but just befriend the world because they are not filled with the Spirit. What if the Lord calls them suddenly? They can't say, "I am not ready yet, so wait for a while" (Matthew 25:1-13). Therefore, we need to pray fervently always and receive fullness of the Holy Spirit.

Ask, Seek, and Knock

"Ask, and it will be given to you;
seek, and you will find;
knock, and it will be opened to you."

(Matthew 7:7)

To Find God

Wind is invisible but we know wind exists because we can feel it on our skin and see things that are moved by the wind. Likewise, we can clearly know that God is alive by seeing His divine nature through what has been made and witnessing evidences that show the living God.

God is spirit, so we can't see Him with naked eyes. But He taught us how to meet Him. Proverbs 8:17 reads, *"I love those who love me; and those who diligently seek me will find me."* Then, how can we find the living God?

Above all, we can find Him in the 66 books of the Bible.

God reveals Himself through the Bible, so we can know His will and heart when we read and understand the Bible. Also Romans 10:17 reads, *"So faith comes from hearing, and hearing by the word of Christ."* Thus, we should go to church where the Word of God is preached. By listening to God's Word diligently, reading the Bible, and realizing the spiritual meaning by the inspiration of the Holy Spirit, we can learn God's heart, get close to Him, and find Him.

Second, we can find Him in prayer.

Jeremiah 29:12-13 says, *"Then you will call upon Me and come and pray to Me, and I will listen to you. You will seek Me and find Me when you search for Me with all your heart."* When we kneel down and cry out in prayer earnestly out of reverence for God, we will find the living God. The forefathers of faith like Moses, Elijah, and the apostle Paul experienced God's amazing works by calling upon God in prayer.

Third, we can find Him in praise.

God accepts praise with great joy. Praise is a form of prayer with melody. It is a way to find God. Therefore, anyone who offers up praise with all his or her heart and mind can find God. Through praise, your sadness changes into joy and you are comforted (Psalm 105:2-3), your broken heart is healed (1 Samuel 16:23), and you receive strength to overcome hardship

(1 Peter 1:3-7).

Fourth, we can find Him in worship services.

In the Old Testament time, people could meet God through sacrifices. Abraham built an altar and gave sacrifice to God everywhere he went, and King Solomon offered Him a thousand burnt offerings. In doing so, they met God and received amazing blessings. The sacrifices in the Old Testament have been changed into services of worship in the New Testament times. So attending the services is also a way to come before God and find Him. When we worship in spirit and truth as recorded in John 4:24, we will be filled with hope for Heaven and joy and we can find God who is life.

Last, we can find Him when we come into goodness, righteousness, light, and love.

God dwells in goodness, righteousness, light, and love. Cornelius was a Gentile but he was a devout man and one who feared God with all his household, and gave many alms to the Jewish people and prayed to God continually. Those who are full of goodness in their hearts give out goodness in words and deeds. God came to Cornelius and gave blessings in which all his household, relatives, and even friends reached salvation. Thus, I hope you will meet the living God by dwelling in the truth.

Worship Service God Accepts

The reason why we should give service to God is that God created the heavens and the earth and all things in them for us and saved us from sins by sending Jesus Christ to us. Genesis 4:3-5 tells us that there are services God doesn't accept while there are services God accepts.

Abel obeyed God's Word giving a sacrifice of blood, so God had regard for him and his offering. But Cain gave a sacrifice that suited his own thoughts, so God had no regard for him or his offering. The same applies today. God delights in spiritual services that are offered according to His will, but He doesn't accept fleshly services that are offered in idle thoughts with no dedication and no joy.

By offering a thousand burnt offerings to God with all his heart, Solomon received a wise and discerning heart, so that there had been no one like him before him, nor should one like him arise after him. Additionally, he received even what he hadn't asked, in riches, honor, and long life (1 Kings 3:1-15). When we also worship in spirit and truth out of love for God (John 4:24), God will accept it with joy and bless us so that we may prosper in all aspects and enjoy good health even as our souls prosper.

You cannot give services God accepts if you attend church just on Sundays. You can say you give services He wants only when your whole life is given to Him as a spiritual service that God acknowledges.

The basis of spiritual services is in 1 Thessalonians 5:16-18, which reads, *"Rejoice always; pray without ceasing; in everything give thanks; for this is God's will for you in Christ Jesus."*

We can rejoice always because Jesus redeemed us as a propitiation for all our sins. He gave us hope for the resurrection and beautiful Heaven by overcoming death. Those who believe this have hope for eternal Heaven and can rejoice no matter what the difficulty might be.

We need to pray without ceasing because prayer is breathing of our souls. Just as men die when they stop breathing, our spirits can't live when we stop praying. Therefore, we should communicate with God with prayer all the time. By doing so, our spirits are full and we can lead a victorious life.

We can give thanks in everything because God is our Father and He promised to give answers to whatever we ask. We should give thanks in everything. When we give thanks even in hardship, God causes everything to work together for good and makes more reasons for which we can give thanks. Thus, we should lead a life of spiritual services that God delights in, by rejoicing always, praying without ceasing, and giving thanks in everything.

God-pleasing Praise

While preaching the gospel, Paul and Silas were imprisoned, but while in the prison they sang hymns of praise to God from the bottom of their hearts. About midnight they were singing and suddenly there came a great earthquake, so that the foundations of the prison house were shaken, and immediately all the doors were opened (Acts 16:25-26). It is in such ways as this that praise has great power to drive away dark forces and move God the Almighty.

In the Bible there are many kinds of artistic works of praise, psalms, songs, performances, and dance, and in all His works they show God's glory and dignity. Psalm 150:3-4 says, *"Praise Him with trumpet sound; praise Him with harp and lyre. Praise Him with timbrel and dancing; praise Him with stringed instruments and pipe."* And Ephesians 5:19 reads, *"Speaking to one another in psalms and hymns and spiritual songs, singing and making melody with your heart to the*

Lord."

Then, what kind of praise does God joyfully accept?

First, God joyfully accepts praise of thanks given with hope for Heaven and joy.

There are praises of repentance in which we repent that we haven't lived in God's Word. There are praises to be offered up in order to fulfill our God-given duties. But, the most joyful praises to God are the ones offered up with hope for Heaven, joy and thanksgiving.

People who see only Heaven and want to give glory to God always long for holy and spiritual things. Through praise they deliver the hope for Heaven that overflows in their hearts to others. God accepts their praises joyfully because they offer their praise with overflowing joy, love for God, and thanksgiving.

Second, God accepts praise given with all the heart.

The praise given with all the heart is given with holy and spotless hearts. God is spotless, blameless, and holy, so He joyfully accepts the praise given by those who have clean hearts with no evil. Furthermore, if they have a neat and tidy appearance while giving praise and devotions, God will be even more pleased with them.

Third, God accepts praise prepared with prayer.

Only when we pray can we become filled with the Spirit and rejoice always and give thanks. And only through prayer can we cast away the lust of the flesh, the lust of the eyes, and the boastful pride of life that come from the world (1 John 2:16). Peace will come upon our hearts and we will become holy. And when this happens we can give praise that God delights in.

Last, God accepts praise given in fullness of the Holy Spirit.

Praise should give grace and move listeners' hearts. To do so, praise givers should be filled with inspiration of the Holy Spirit first and give beautiful and gracious praise. When they praise God in fullness of the Spirit, God will accept it with joy and the heavenly hosts and angels will reply. God's love and blessing will come upon them and precious rewards will be piled up in Heaven.

Jesus Provided Us with a Good Example of Prayer

Prayer is the most important basic action in a Christian life. This is because through prayer we can communicate with God, receive answers to our prayers, receive heavenly strength and wisdom, and lead a victorious life. On the contrary, when we don't pray, we can't lead a proper Christian life and our spirit and soul lose strength. That's why we call prayer 'the breathing of our spirit.'

God gave us a promise saying in Mark 11:24, *"Therefore I say to you, all things for which you pray and ask, believe that you have received them, and they will be granted you."* So it's natural to receive answers when we pray, but some don't receive answers although they ask diligently. Then, they should check their prayers in comparison with Jesus' prayer. Let's look at how Jesus prayed.

First, Jesus prayed habitually.

Jesus habitually went up to the Mount of Olives and prayed (Luke 22:39). Jesus' disciples, Peter and John went up to the Temple at a regular hour and prayed (Acts 3:1) and Daniel prayed with windows open towards Jerusalem three times a day (Daniel 6:10). We have to keep in our hearts that to pray habitually without ceasing is God's will (1 Thessalonians 5:17-18) and watch and pray as His children.

Second, Jesus knelt down in prayer.

Luke 22:41 describes Jesus praying on bended knees before the crucifixion. The forefathers of faith like Elijah who brought down fire and the apostle Paul knelt down in prayer (1 Kings 18:42; Acts 20:36). When we kneel down we can be more focused on our hearts. The act of kneeling down itself shows one's reverent respect for God, so it's natural that we should kneel down in prayer before God the Creator.

Third, Jesus prayed according to God's will.

When Jesus prayed in Gethsemane, He said *"Father, if You are willing, remove this cup from Me; yet not My will, but Yours be done"* (Luke 22:42). LLike Him, we should also follow God's will, not seeking our own benefits and commit everything to God in prayer. Committing everything to God in prayer is to believe that God is the One who causes all things to work together for good and gives only good things to His children and to give thanks and rejoice for all things regardless of situations.

Fourth, Jesus prayed very fervently in agony.

Luke 22:44 says, *"And being in agony He was praying very fervently; and His sweat became like drops of blood, falling down upon the ground."* Jesus prayed in this way in Gethsemane the night before His crucifixion.

After Adam's disobedience, men came to eat bread only by the sweat of their brows as explained in Genesis 3:17-19. In other words, we need to work with the sweat of our faces to gain something. But, when we ask God for things that are not obtainable with our own strength, then how much more fervently should we pray to receive them? Therefore, I hope you will receive answers to whatever you pray for by praying habitually, with attitudes that God wants, following God's will, and praying fervently like Jesus.

Ask, Seek, and Knock

Just as parents want to give their beloved children good things, the God of love wants to give the best things to us who are His children. However, under the spiritual law He can't give answers unless we ask. So, He says in Matthew 7:7, *"Ask, and it will be given to you; seek, and you will find; knock, and it will be opened to you."*

What should we ask for?

Above all, we should ask to see the LORD and His face, and to receive His strength (Psalm 105:4). Only when God gives us grace and strength from above can we overcome the world and live in the Word of God. To live according to the Word, we need faith first. Therefore, to receive God's strength is to ask Him to give us faith.

To ask to see God's face is to try hard to know about God.

It means that those who didn't believe in God came to open the door to their minds, seek God, get to know Him, and ask to hear His voice. John 1:1 tells us that God is the Word, so to understand and realize the spiritual meanings of the 66 books of the Bible is to see God's face.

Next, we need to ask to accomplish God's kingdom and His righteousness (Matthew 6:33). More souls will receive salvation and God's kingdom will be extended more to the extent that we diligently preach about Jesus Christ. Thus, to accomplish God's kingdom is to pray for national and world evangelism so that all people reach salvation. Accomplishing His righteousness is also to pray to come into light from darkness by understanding the Word of God, resembling God who is holy, and becoming sanctified.

We also need to ask for strength to fulfill God-given duties as workers (1 Corinthians 4:2). We have to pray to become workers for God's kingdom, and if we are already His workers, we should pray to fulfill the duties well. That is, we should ask for strength not only to fulfill our own duties, but also to do a great job even when more important and difficult jobs are given.

Furthermore, we should ask for our daily bread (Matthew 6:11). It means that we need to ask for necessary clothing, food, and shelter, blessing in our businesses, good health of family members, and financial blessings. God already redeemed us from all poverty and diseases through Jesus Christ so that we can enjoy blessings in our lives. Therefore, after asking to accomplish God's kingdom and righteousness, we also need to ask to God for the necessities in our lives so that we can enjoy rich, healthy, and prosperous lives.

Then, what should we seek?

Here, to 'seek' means that we have to seek the lost image of God. Adam, the first man, was created as a living spirit in God's image. But by disobeying what God had told him to do, Adam took the way of death—which is the wages of sin—and he lost the image of God. Thus, we have to recover the lost image of God. When we accept Jesus Christ and receive the Holy Spirit as a gift, our dead spirits are revived and we can recover the image of God.

Lastly, what should we knock on?

This tells us to receive answers by knocking on God's heart. To do so, we have to keep God's Word and please Him. When God is pleased, He will open the heavenly gates and pour down answers and blessings upon us.

The Prayer of Faith, Prayer of Love, and the Prayer of a Righteous Man

Prayer is a key to answers and blessings. When we move God's heart with prayer, answers and blessings will come upon us. Then, what kind of prayer can result in quickly giving us answers?

First of all, it is a prayer of faith.

In Exodus 17:8-16 Moses could achieve a victory in the battle between Israel and Amalek through his prayer of faith. By the prayer of Joshua, the sun and the moon stood still almost all day (Joshua 10:13). Also, Elijah's earnest prayer brought fire down from above (1 Kings 18:38). Like in these examples, those who pray with faith and with no doubt at all can experience God's amazing works.

Second, it is a prayer of love.

Fleshly love seeks personal benefit and it becomes corrupt over time. On the other hand, spiritual love seeks the benefit of others and is willing to make self-sacrifices. It never changes, even after extended passage of time. If you have spiritual love, you love your neighbors as yourself. You can regard others' problems as though they were your own, and you can ask for what others want in their personal situations. God listens to such prayers of true love and gives answers to them quickly.

Third, it is the prayer of a righteous man.

The prayer of a righteous man refers to prayer we offer with a good and beautiful heart that resembles the Lord's heart and it is the prayer that earnestly asks according to God's will. On the journey from Egypt to the land of Canaan, the Israelites disobeyed God's Word and made a calf of molten gold and worshipped it. God was furious, so He told Moses that He would destroy them and make of Moses a great nation. But Moses asked of God in prayer to relent and not to destroy them. He offered his own life as security for theirs. God changed His mind and didn't destroy them. God valued Moses who resembled Him more than millions of the Israelites and gave answers to his prayer. Namely, *"the effective prayer of a righteous man can accomplish much"* (James 5:16).

Seek God's Kingdom and His Righteousness

In the Bible are many passages about prayer. Matthew 6:33 says, *"But seek first His kingdom and His righteousness, and all these things will be added to you."* God wants us to seek first His kingdom and His righteousness when we pray.

Then, what does it mean to seek God's kingdom?

It means to pray for souls' salvation by preaching the gospel. The resurrected Lord gave His Great Commission to His disciples before He ascended into Heaven. It is in Acts 1:8 saying, *"But you will receive power when the Holy Spirit has come upon you; and you shall be My witnesses both in Jerusalem, and in all Judea and Samaria, and even to the remotest part of the earth."*

The Lord died on the cross to take the sins of mankind, who were destined to destruction as servants of the enemy devil and Satan. On the third day after He died, He overcame death and resurrected. By this, those who accept Jesus Christ and believe in His name can receive forgiveness and gain the right to become God's children. In the end they can reach salvation. Therefore, to the extent that we preach Jesus Christ, the camp of the enemy devil and Satan is destroyed and God's kingdom is fulfilled. By knowing this, we should pray for preaching the gospel. Prayers for churches, pastors, constructing sanctuaries, church workers, and the world evangelism fall under this category of prayer.

Next, what does it mean to seek God's righteousness?

It means that we should pray to become righteous men who resemble the Lord and act according to God's Word. 1 Peter 1:16 reads, *"Because it is written, 'You shall be holy, for I am holy.'"* And Matthew 5:48 says, *"Therefore you are to be perfect, as your heavenly Father is perfect."* Therefore, we as God's children should pray fervently to achieve righteousness in our hearts completely.

A Man for Whom Nothing Is Impossible

Today science and medicine have achieved remarkable developments, but still there are a lot of things that can't be done with human power. However, there is nothing impossible in faith because within faith it is not human power but only the power of God the Almighty that works. The Bible records countless evidences so that people can believe in the world of faith where nothing is impossible. The Bible also tells us the kind of people who were able to experience the world of faith and for what traits of them God acknowledges them as men of faith and gave answers and blessings.

Just as said in Mark 9:23 reading, *"And Jesus said to him, '"If You can?" All things are possible to him who believes,'"* there should be nothing impossible for those who truly believe in God. Then, what kind of persons have nothing impossible in faith?

First, they don't have a wall of sins before God.

Isaiah 59:1-2 reads, *"Behold, the LORD's hand is not so short that it cannot save; nor is His ear so dull that it cannot hear. But your iniquities have made a separation between you and your God."* If a wall of sins exists between us and God, we can't receive answers and realize God's will. If we cannot realize His will we can't obey His will. Therefore, if we have a wall of sins we should destroy the wall quickly by repenting thoroughly.

Second, they follow God's will.

Matthew 22:37 reads, *"You shall love the LORD your God with all your heart, and with all your soul, and with all your mind."* Thus, we must not do things that are against God's will even if we like them. Also, we must do something even if we hate it as long as it is God's will. When we follow His will with all our hearts, souls, and minds, He will give us perfect faith.

Third, they please God by loving Him.

John 14:21 reads, *"He who has My commandments and keeps them is the one who loves Me; and he who loves Me will be loved by My Father, and I will love him and will disclose Myself to him."* If we love God, keep His commandments, and do all to the glory of God whether we eat or drink or whatever we do, then God is pleased with us and gives us faith in which we can do things that are impossible with human power. Therefore, by pleasing God all the time, I hope you will lead a life in which nothing is impossible in faith and give glory to God whatever you do.

Prayer in Agreement with the Holy Spirit

Jesus taught His disciples how to receive answers to their prayers. Among them, one of the ways is written in Matthew 18:19. It says, *"Again I say to you, that if two of you agree on earth about anything that they may ask, it shall be done for them by My Father who is in heaven."* Prayer of agreement refers to prayer given with one heart. Why is this kind of prayer powerful?

"Two of you agree on earth about anything that they may ask" spiritually indicates that we pray being united as one with the Holy Spirit. It doesn't matter that we pray alone or with more than two people. "The prayer given in unification with the Spirit" is described in this passage as "two of you agree on earth about anything that they may ask." When we accept Jesus Christ, the Holy Spirit comes into our hearts and revives our spirits that were dead due to sins. In the hearts of God's children, the Spirit dwells and leads them to the truth. The Holy Spirit has the heart of God and searches the depths of God (1 Corinthians 2:10). And He prays for believers according to God's will (Romans 8:27). Thus, when we pray in the guidance of the Holy Spirit, God will accept our prayer with joy and give answers to whatever we ask.

Then, what should we do to pray in unity with the Holy Spirit all the time?

Our hearts should be changed into the truth, namely, the hearts of spirit. To the extent that we keep God's Word and change into spirit, the Spirit guides us more clearly and lets us hear His voice. By doing so, He allows us to know God's will. When we hear the voice of the Spirit and receive His guidance and obey Him, we will be filled with the Holy Spirit and we can become united as one with Him.

If we pray with one heart with the Spirit in this way, the prayer will become very powerful. Even if just one person is united with the Spirit in prayer, great works can take place. Then, if a lot of people gather and give such prayers, how much more powerful the prayer will be! Therefore, I hope you will experience God's astounding works by praying in agreement with the Spirit when hardship comes to your church, family, workplace, or businesses.

Fasting and Prayer that Delights God

One day, a man came to Jesus' disciples to ask them to cure his epileptic son who was demon-possessed. But they couldn't cure him. Jesus told them to bring him to Him and then Jesus rebuked the demon, and it came out of him. Seeing this, the disciples asked why they couldn't heal him. Jesus said this was because of the littleness of their faith (Matthew 17:20), and He also said *"This kind cannot come out by anything but prayer"* (Mark 9:29). Therefore, we should pray to receive healing of diseases and solutions to problems. In particular, we can receive answers quickly when we pray earnestly with fasting.

In the Bible are many people who received answers and blessings through prayer with fasting. Esther saved her people with her three-day fast. The people of Nineveh, who had been on the way of destruction due to sins, turned from their ways with fasting and finally received salvation. Prayer with fasting is really powerful in this way.

God gave a promise in Isaiah 58:6-9 saying, *"Is this not the fast which I choose, to loosen the bonds of wickedness, to undo the bands of the yoke, and to let the oppressed go free and break every yoke? Is it not to divide your bread with the hungry and bring the homeless poor into the house; when you see the naked, to cover him; and not to hide yourself from your own flesh? Then your light will break out like the dawn, and your recovery will speedily spring forth; and your righteousness will go before you; the glory of the LORD will be your rear guard. Then you will call, and the LORD will answer; you will cry, and He will say, 'Here I am.'"*

Praying with fasting is not to eat anything except for water and earnestly ask God for answers with strong determination saying "If I die, I die."

When giving fasting, we need to cry out in prayer with spiritual love and stay away from any worldly pleasure (Isaiah 58:3-5). The duration varies from a meal-fasting, one day, two-day, three-day, five-day, seven-day fasting, to more than seven days. But if you fast for more than ten days, you must not make your decision for such a fast easily. You must receive the guidance of the Holy Spirit according to God's will for such a fast.

After fasting, you should have recovery meals. Only after you have appropriate recovery meals, you can say you finish fasting properly. During the recovery meals, you still have to ask God for your prayer titles in the ways God wants. The one thing we should be aware of is that trials might come after fasting. Therefore, to drive away trials with faith, we should prepare for it with prayer and we must not take in any worldly pleasure and not become angry. When we do it properly, God will give us answers and blessing at the most appropriate time in His ways.

Unchanging Heart
that Fulfills a Vow

Even though they made a firm promise, people will often break their promise if they think it won't be of benefit to them. They change their plans frequently according to situations. They tend to keep promises they regard important but easily break promises for which they have little regard. If you neglect small things and promises, over time you will become dull in keeping the important promises. Such people cannot gain trust from God as well as trust in relationships with other people.

Those who truly fear God keep promises not only made with others, but also with themselves. They also fulfill those promises before God for sure.

Deuteronomy 23:21-23 says, *"When you make a vow to the LORD your God, you shall not delay to pay it, for it would be sin in you, and the LORD your God will surely require it of you. However, if you refrain from vowing, it would not be sin in you. You shall be careful to perform what goes out from your lips, just as you have voluntarily vowed to the LORD your God, what you have promised."* If you don't perform what you vowed to God, it will become a great wall of sin against God because it is to mock Him. But God gives answers quickly to those who keep what they vowed.

Jephthah made a vow to God, before the battle against the sons of Ammon, for the victory of Israel. *"If You will indeed give the sons of Ammon into my hand, then it shall be that whatever comes out of the doors of my house to meet me when I return in peace from the sons of Ammon, it shall be the LORD's, and I will offer it up as a burnt offering"* (Judges 11:30-31). God answered his vowed prayer and gave victory to the Israelites. Jephthat returned home with joy.

But the first one who came out of the doors of his house to meet him was his only daughter. She came to meet him, dancing with tambourines. She looked lovely. Seeing her, Jephthah said, *"Alas, my daughter! You have brought me very low, and you are among those who trouble me; for I have given my word to the LORD, and I cannot take it back"* (Judges 11:35).

He valued his vow before God more than his beloved daughter's life so he did as he had spoken. God answers prayer of those who have honesty and not falsehood in their hearts. So, we should ask Him with sincere hearts and keep any vows made before God.

Life of Walking with God

God stays with those who act according to God's will and protects them. Jesus said in John 8:29, *"And He who sent Me is with Me; He has not left Me alone, for I always do the things that are pleasing to Him."* Because Jesus always pleased God in all things, God walked with Jesus so that He could fulfill God's will completely. Then, how could Jesus receive such blessings?

First, Jesus humbled Himself and unconditionally obeyed God.

As said in John 1:3, *"All things came into being through Him, and apart from Him nothing came into being that has come into being,"* Jesus is one with God the Creator. But, He did not regard equality with God. He rather took the form of a bond-servant and came to the earth to fulfill God's will and

He humbled Himself by becoming obedient to the point of death—even to be crucified by the hands of sinners. So God said to Jesus who obeyed Him, *"This is My beloved Son, in whom I am well-pleased"* (Matthew 3:17). He prepared everything for Jesus and worked for Him.

Second, Jesus accepted God's will completely and practiced it.

1 Peter 2:22-23 says, *"[Christ] committed no sin, nor was any deceit found in His mouth; and while being reviled, He did not revile in return; while suffering, He uttered no threats, but kept entrusting Himself to Him who judges righteously."* And Philippians 2:8 reads, *"Being found in appearance as a man, He humbled Himself by becoming obedient to the point of death, even death on a cross."* We can know by these things that Jesus acted only according to God's will.

Third, Jesus acted only relying on the Word of God.

When devil tried to tempt Jesus, He passed all the temptations by relying on the Word of God (Matthew 4:1-11). In Matthew chapter 26, Judas came up accompanied by a large crowd who came from the chief priests and elders of the people to capture Jesus. Then, Peter struck the man of the high priest and cut off his ear. Jesus said to him, *"'Do you think that I cannot appeal to My Father, and He will at once put at My disposal more than twelve legions of angels? How then will the Scriptures be fulfilled, which say that it must happen this way?' And Jesus said to the people who came to capture Him, 'But all this has taken place to fulfill the Scriptures of the prophets'"* (Matthew 26:53-54).

He accomplished God's will perfectly by acting on the Word of God no matter what the circumstance. When we follow God-pleasing will like Jesus did, God will always be with us.

Part 3

Answers Come from God

"Whatever you ask in My name,
that will I do,
so that the Father may be glorified
in the Son."

(John 14:13)

The Law of Hope

Jacob and Esau were twin brothers. The older one, Esau, was a hunter, and the younger one, Jacob, dwelt in tents and helped his mother. Jacob was a great dreamer from the time he was young. One day, Jacob made lentil stew. Esau came in from hunting in the fields and he was faint with hunger. He asked Jacob to feed him with some of the stew. Jacob told him to sell his birthright to him in return for some of the stew. Esau agreed and sold his birthright to Jacob for momentary satisfaction.

It came to pass, that when Isaac was old, he called Esau, his eldest son. He told Esau to get some venison and make him savory food and then he said he would bless him. Rebekah, Isaac's wife, heard this. She decided to deceive her husband, whose eyes were dim, and allow for her second son, Jacob, to receive the blessing of the first son. Esau later found out that Jacob had taken his blessing away, and decided to kill Jacob.

Jacob left his hometown for Haran where his uncle Laban lived. After he served Laban diligently, he told Laban he was going to return home. But Laban asked Jacob, who was diligent and wise, to remain with him a little longer and appointed his wages. Jacob said that that day he would pass through all Laban's flocks of sheep and remove from them all the speckled or spotted and all the dark-colored lambs among the sheep, and the spotted and speckled among the goats: and of such was to be his compensation. There was no reason for Laban to reject it because he knew it was more beneficial to him.

Why did Jacob give such suggestion? God watched Laban who sought his own greed and benefit and Jacob who had served with him sincerely. So God gave wisdom to Jacob so that he could receive blessing. Jacob took fresh rods of poplar and almond and plane trees, and peeled white stripes in them, exposing the white which was in the rods. And He set the rods which he had peeled in front of the flocks in the gutters, even in the watering troughs, where the flocks came to drink; and they mated when they came to drink, that they should see the rods when they conceived or when they came to drink. Surprisingly, they conceived and gave birth to the spotted and the speckled as they saw the rods.

Jacob put the rods only when the stronger of the sheep and the goats were mating. This way, the stronger among the young became Jacob's and the weaker Laban's. This is what is called

"Hope of Spring" or "the Law of Hope."

Just as said in Hebrews 11:1, *"Now faith is the assurance of things hoped for,"* things hoped for are not visible in present but they will be realized when we keep the hope.

What do you hope for? God's children should hope for eternal Heaven. So you have to pray for your souls to be prosperous, act according to God's Word, cast away evil, and resemble the Lord. You need to look forward to blessings God will give with eyes of faith in businesses, workplaces, and family. When you want your family or your children to change, you also have to see them with faith and follow goodness and the truth. Then, God will fulfill your heart's desires in accordance with your faith.

To Fulfill Our Heart's Desire

There is a story of a magic lamp. When a person rubs the lamp three times, a genie comes out and fulfills three desires of his heart. This is a story that men made up, but it is basically possible for those who are God's children. Anyone who believes in God and acts according to His Word can receive answers to his or her prayers. We can receive them not only three times, but as many times as we want. Then, how can we lead a Christian life in which our heart's desires are fulfilled?

First, we need to check our hearts.

Some people used to believe in superstition or their own ability or talents, but they come to find God only when they are faced with some problems that they can never solve. Some others just have a vague hope that they might solve their problems when they pray. Still others even doubt thinking,

"Will it be really answered?" God looks at our inner hearts, so we need to check our hearts to receive answers. We should check if we really believe in God or we doubt or have expectations of some kind of 'luck'. Only when we come to God with faith can we receive answers.

Second, we need to check if we have assurance of salvation.

If you believe from your heart that God raised Him from the dead and confess with your mouth Jesus as the Lord, you will gain the right to become God's children and the assurance of salvation will come to you (Romans 10:9-10). Those who have such assurance of salvation naturally follow God's will and God will fulfill their desires of heart. If there is no answer for you from God although you pray, you need to check if you have the assurance of salvation. Also, you should check if you have wall of sins against God. If you have done something against the Word of God, only after you repent, can you receive answers to what you pray for.

Third, we need to show deeds that are pleasing to God.

As a child grows up he learns how to please his parents.

Likewise, we can please God to the extent that we realize the truth. Psalm 37:4 says, *"Delight yourself in the LORD; and He will give you the desires of your heart."* Here, "Delight yourself in the LORD" means that we should enjoy God-given joy that is true, namely, spiritual joy. To do so, we have to please God.

God is pleased with service and prayer given with the heart, good deeds, charitable works, offerings, gospel preaching, and praise singing (Psalm 51:19; Psalm 69:30-31; Acts 10:4; 2 Corinthians 9:7; 1 Thessalonians 2:4). Above all, He delights in our faith (Hebrews 11:6). When we please God with perfect deeds of faith, God will fulfill our heart's desires even if we just harbor them in our hearts.

Positive Words of Faith

People speak many words even a day. They encourage others with gentle words or hurt their feeling with harsh words. Some fall in hardship because of words they blurt out. In the Bible, many forefathers received answers by giving confessions of faith.

God told the Israelites many times that He would give them the land of Canaan flowing with milk and honey. One day, the Israelites sent twelve spies to scout the land before entering the land of Canaan. Ten of them gave negative reports, and eventually died in the wilderness, but Joshua and Caleb gave positive reports because they believed in God the Almighty. In doing so, they entered the land of Canaan (Numbers 14:7-9, 30). Like them, those who have true faith don't blame something on the environment but just see the power of God and keep saying positive words. Why then does an answer depend on the profession of lips?

First, the Holy Spirit works in the confession of faith.

The Holy Spirit who dwells in us is pleased when we praise God, pray, and speak words of faith. When we do things that are pleasing to the Spirit, we can experience His power. When we give thanks for the grace of salvation of Jesus Christ always and say the words of faith, we can receive answers to everything we ask for in the works of the Holy Spirit.

Second, words can change us.

The control center for speech of a person's body also controls all nerves of the body. That's why one's personality or his life is changed by what he says. The Bible says that words are like the bit in a horse's mouth and the rudder of a ship. It also compares it to a small fire that sets a forest aflame (James 3:2-6).

People put bits into horses' mouth to control their direction and movement. Likewise, human's destiny depends on a small tongue in his or her mouth. This is why the Bible likens bits for horses to the words from our lips. Just as recorded in Proverbs 18:21, *"Death and life are in the power of the tongue, and those who love it will eat its fruit,"* we should realize how much a single one of our words could affect our life.

God abides with those who practice the truth, so when we keep His Word that is the truth, He will manifest amazing works (Romans 10:8-10). But negative words or words of resentment and lamentation disturb the works of the Spirit. Therefore, do not say "It's impossible" or "It's difficult". But say *"I can do all things through Him who strengthens me"* (Philippians 4:13). By doing so, I hope you will experience God's works all the time.

Give Thanks to the Lord

Jehoshaphat was the fourth king of Southern Judah and he loved God. One day, it came about after this that the sons of Moab and the sons of Ammon came to wage a war against Jehoshaphat. He proclaimed a fast throughout all Judah and sought help from God. After receiving answer from God that He would give victory to him, he rejoiced together with his people and praised God. Next day, he appointed those who sang to God and had them in holy attire, and made them go out before the army and praise God.

God worked for the people of Judah who showed faith under such an urgent situation, so their enemies destroyed one another. When Jehoshaphat and his people came to take their spoil, they found goods, garments and valuable things more than they could carry. And it took them three days to take the spoil because there was so much.

If we rejoice, give thanks, and rely on God when we encounter difficulties like Jehoshaphat did, trials will go away and blessings will come upon us. Then, why should we give thanks to God in such situations?

First, because He makes the impossible possible for us

The best way to getting out of desperate situation is to give thanks to God. Thanksgiving to God is a key to bringing God's great power down from above. Paul and Silas didn't complain nor grudge when they were imprisoned for the sake of their gospel-preaching. Rather they gave thanks and praised God. Then, a great earthquake suddenly came and shook the foundations of the prison house. At the same time all the doors were opened and everyone's chains were unfastened (Acts chapter 16).

The enemy devil and Satan prowl around like a roaring lion, seeking someone to devour and make us complain. But when we believe God who makes nothing impossible and give thanks to Him, He will make everything prosperous for us.

Second, because in everything giving thanks is God's will

Ephesians 5:20 reads, *"Always giving thanks for all things in the name of our Lord Jesus Christ to God, even the Father."* Therefore, we should give thanks to God always in any situation. 'Any situation' includes not only favorable situations but also hardship as well. We can give thanks even for the hardship because we believe that our good God will be with us forever and because we also believe God who causes all things to work together for good (Romans 8:28).

Third, because He gives us everlasting hope for Heaven

Those who believe Jesus Christ can rejoice and give thanks under any circumstance because they have God-given hope for Heaven. How happy and thankful it is that we received a promise that we will live in the beauty of Heaven forever—where there is no tear, no sorrow, no pain, and no death after the life in this world stained with sin and evil ends!

Fourth, because God is always with us

While the sun and rains are equally given by God's grace to all people, God's protection in accidents and danger is special grace given only to God's children. When they take a wrong way, God gives His beloved children realization so that they can turn away from the wrong way. If they don't turn away, He sometimes gives them punishments. But this is also in the love of God who wants to lead them to the way of life, so they can give thanks to God. Offering thanksgiving to God is His will, a key to the miracle which changes impossible things into possible things, and a shortcut to blessings. So I hope you will give thanks no matter what the situation may be.

Those who Wait for the Lord

There are some people who enjoy prosperity, but still at times they are faced with hardship. They often feel frustrated and lose heart because the problems are so hard to solve. The Bible tells us the way to gain new strength in any case or situation.

Isaiah 40:31 says, *"Yet those who wait for the LORD will gain new strength; they will mount up with wings like eagles, they will run and not get tired, they will walk and not become weary."* When we become a person who waits for the LORD, God will not leave us alone, but He will give us strength and power so that we can solve difficult problems. Let's delve in the characteristics of those who wait for the LORD.

First, they stay close to the Word of God

To 'wait' for God means to desire to meet the living God

earnestly. Therefore, those who wait for the LORD enjoy reading and listening to the Word of God and putting it in their hearts. They also like to act according to it. Because the Word of God contains the heart and the will of God, they keep and practice the Word. They will be like the tree firmly planted by streams of water, which yields its fruit in its season and its leaf does not wither—in whatever they do, they prosper.

Second, they communicate with God in prayer

The forefathers of faith communicated with God in prayer. Abraham built an altar wherever he went and prayed to God. In return, he always enjoyed a prosperous life. Daniel valued prayer more than his own life (Daniel chapters 7-12). So, he was able to see amazing visions and receive revelation from God. Elijah received answer of rains in three-year-and-a-half severe drought through prayer (1 Kings chapter 18). Like them, when we call out to God in prayer without ceasing, we can have deep communication with God and we will be provided with power and strength from above.

Third, they commit everything to God

God lets them hear the voice of the Spirit and shows them the proper way to take. Nevertheless, if they insist on their own will, they can't experience the works of the Spirit. Proverbs 16:3 says, *"Commit your works to the LORD and your plans will be established."* So we need to commit our works to God. We will experience His amazing touch when we commit everything to God and pray without worrying before any difficulties (Philippians 4:6).

Fourth, those who wait for the LORD are earnest in everything

Being earnest means that you do your best in everything in your charge with sincere heart and no dishonesty. That is, you do everything as if you do your own work and you do it with all your heart. Daniel and Joseph were always earnest and diligent under any situation and followed the right way. In the end, God raised them up to the position where they were praised by the people.

Even today, those who wait for God don't lose heart in any situation but rely on God and work diligently knowing that they can achieve victory with God's power even in hardship and trials.

True Relief

Water pours out of a well only as much as we pump. Likewise, when we give what we have like money, knowledge, and skill to others, we can be repaid with more than what we give. We find in Exodus 22:22, Deuteronomy 14:29, and James 1:27 that God wants us to have mercy towards orphans and widows and take care of them. Because He is delighted in children who have and give love to their neighbors, He gives them blessings both in spirit and body and greatly rewards them in Heaven.

Then, what kind of help does God want us to give others?

1 John 3:18 says, *"Let us not love with word or with tongue, but in deed and truth."* Jesus also told us not to let our left hand know what our right hand is doing so that our giving

will be in secret (Matthew 6:3-4). We have to give help to the poor with a humble heart. We should help people not only when we enjoy wealth to some degree. Just as an old Korean saying goes, "Share even a bean with your neighbor", we should share even a small thing with our neighbors out of love for them under any circumstance.

However, some suffer from hardship because they gave aid to those whom they should not have helped. In part, we should not help those who lead idle lives though they are healthy enough to provide for themselves in the course of their own lives (2 Thessalonians 3:10). When we help them, it stops them from becoming independent. Also, we must not help those who fall into hardship due to their sins. God's will is for them to realize their sins and turn away from them and lead proper Christian lives. So, in such a case we will suffer together with them if we help them.

Therefore, we should first help our brothers and sisters who can't provide for their own lives due to accidents or diseases. We should help orphans, widows, and students who have no head-of-the-household in the family to provide for them and can't support themselves. When we help and give aid to people in God's will and love, God, who searches in all things, will bless us in return.

Sincerity of a Thousand Burnt Offerings

A saying goes, "True sincerity moves heaven." It means heaven is moved by wholehearted sincerity. In other words, we can produce good outcomes when we put efforts in anything with honest sincerity. The Bible talks about many figures that experienced God's works through their sincerity that moved God and people around them.

Solomon was the king of Israel as a successor to King David. Solomon loved God and after he became the king, in his love he offered up a thousand burnt offerings to God.

A burnt offering is the most common way of sacrifice in the Old Testament time. It was to burn animals brought as offerings with fire on the altar. This sacrifice indicates giving our life to God, and keeping all commandments God gave to men. That is, it symbolizes our perfect sacrifice, dedication, and voluntary service before God the Creator.

After Solomon offered up a thousand burnt offerings, God was very pleased and said to him, "Ask what you wish Me to give you." Solomon did not ask for wealth or fame. He asked only for wisdom with which he could rule over His people well. He knew that wisdom was the most necessary thing for him to possess as a king.

God was delighted in him, and gave him not only wisdom but also riches and honor. We can also receive great blessings like Solomon's when we give services and offerings with all our hearts to God and please Him, not seeking our own benefits.

The Reasons We Can't Receive Answers

God's children should always lead a life of giving glory to God (1 Corinthians 10:31). But some Christians look like they are leading a proper Christian life on the outside, but they are far from living a life that gives glory to God. That's why even though they pray, blessings and answers are not received. This is because unlike people, God searches the hearts of men and then gives answers (Proverbs 16:2). So, again, what are the specific reasons why we can't receive answers?

First, it is because we complain and begrudge when we are faced with problems

There are some people who, in general, do keep God's Word. But, they speak negative words when something doesn't agree with what they think and feel. This shows that their hearts haven't been changed into the truth yet. Just as said in Matthew 12:35, *"The good man brings out of his good treasure what is good; and the evil man brings out of his evil treasure what is evil,"* we should pray diligently to have a good heart because our words come from our hearts.

Complaints from our lips return to us like a boomerang, and cause troubles. But people don't know why the troubles came to them because after a while, *they tend to forget what they said.* Thus, we should be careful about what we say, and we should use words of goodness and words of the truth.

Second, it is because we pass judgment and condemnation on those who live according to the Word

Some people don't receive answers because they pass judgment and condemnation on others when they can't understand them or they feel like they are lacking something. So we must not give hard times to others or judge and condemn them even if they don't keep God's Word well. This is because James 4:11 tells us *"Do not speak against one another, brethren. He who speaks against a brother or judges his brother, speaks against the law and judges the law…"*

Third, it is because we have outbursts of anger and enmity towards others when their ideas do not agree with ours

When something does not agree with them some people tend to react to it by frowning, or more overtly, they raise their voice and may get angry at a certain point. What's worse is that they harbor a kind of hatred toward others and they even hold enmity toward them. Matthew 5:39-40 reads, *"Whoever slaps you on your right cheek, turn the other to him also. If anyone wants to sue you and take your shirt, let him have your coat also."* So we should forgive all people with love and mercy.

If answers haven't yet come even though you found the shortcomings listed above and have turned away from them, it means that God is giving you time to pile up faith and good deeds! Thus, when you rejoice and give thanks with unchanging faith, God will give you whatever you ask including good heath, wealth, and fame.

When You Obey Relying on the Word

It happened when Jesus came to Lake Gennesaret. There were two empty boats, and the fishermen had gotten out of them and were washing their nets. Jesus taught the people from Peter's boat. Then, to give blessing to him, He said to Peter, *"Put out into the deep water and let down your nets for a catch"* (Luke 5:4).

As a fisherman, Peter knew how to fish better than almost anyone else. He had already worked hard all night and caught nothing, so it was not easy to obey. But, he went out and let down the nets relying on the Jesus' word. Then, they enclosed a great quantity of fish, and their nets began to break. This happened because Peter obeyed Jesus' words.

When we rely on the Word and obey like Peter, amazing blessings will come upon us. Then, what kind of blessings can we receive when we obey?

First, we can have peace.

The main reason a person does not have peace is the result of seeking personal advantage and benefits. When a person is obsessed with his own thoughts and ideas, he encounters many conflicts. The Word of God is the truth and those who obey it can have peace with others because, they have compassion and consideration for others and serve them without seeking personal benefit. When we become men of the truth who live in the Word of God, we can have peace not only with God, but also with all people and enjoy peaceful and happy lives.

Second, in obedience, the problem of disease is solved

The Bible tells us diseases come from sins (Deuteronomy chapter 28). When God's children don't act by His Word it is the sin of disobedience. When they commit sins, the Father can't protect them and diseases can come to them. He said if they do what is right in God's sight and keep all His statutes, He will put none of the diseases on them that affected Egypt (Exodus 15:26). Like this, when you dwell perfectly in God's Word, God will protect you and diseases will not come upon you. Even if you come down with some disease, you can experience His healing works when you destroy the wall of sins against God.

Third, we can solve the problems of finance.

In Genesis chapter 12, when God told Abraham to go forth to the land which He would show him, Abraham obeyed and left right away. In Hebrews 11:17-19 we see that Abraham again obeyed God even when God told him to give Isaac, whom he had gained at the age of 100, as a burnt offering. He also believed that after he offered up Isaac, God would revive him. God gave Abraham wealth, fame, and authority on the earth as well as spiritual blessing. Therefore, anyone who acts with reliance on God's Word with faith can receive all blessings that Abraham, the forefather of faith enjoyed (Galatians 3:9).

"And He said,
'If you will give earnest heed
to the voice of the LORD your God,
and do what is right in His sight,
and give ear to His commandments,
and keep all His statutes,
I will put none of the diseases on you
which I have put on the Egyptians;
for I, the LORD, am your healer.'"

(Exodus 15:26)

Causes and Healing of Diseases

Many people spend their money and time on dietary therapy or exercise to keep in good shape. Of course, such things are beneficial for us in many ways. But, people are not perfectly free from diseases in these ways, no matter how hard they try. Although they expend such efforts, many of them just wait for death with incurable diseases. But the Bible tells us the causes and healing methods of all diseases and it holds the keys to enjoying good health. What is the cause of diseases and what are the healing methods?

First, diseases are mostly caused by sins

In Exodus 15:26 God said He would put none of the diseases on us if we 'give earnest heed to the voice of God, do what is right in His sight, and give ear to His commandments'. To heal a paralytic, Jesus said to him, *"Son, your sins are forgiven"* (Mark 2:5). That said, not keeping the Word of God then is sin and disease comes from such sins. Therefore, when we destroy the wall of sins, we can be healed of our diseases.

Second, diseases come from things that are considered sins in God's sight—even though people don't consider it to be sin

Some people say they come down with certain diseases even though they didn't commit sins. Do you think it is true? Let's say you are sick because you overate. Overeating belongs to sin because it means you didn't exercise self-control over greed that is gluttony. If you are sick because you eat irregularly or you overwork this is also the result of the lack of self-control by failing to act in accordance with the word of truth. Not following the order of natural law that God has given to us is sin.

Third, some diseases come from nervous problems or mental problems

Hard-feelings don't arise when we understand, forgive, and love others. If you don't have hatred or hot-tempered reactions, your nerves are never negatively stimulated. But if you have evil and don't live in the truth, you will have negative feelings or adverse nervous reaction leading to nervousness, and then that in turn leads to neurogenic or mental diseases. Some look fine outwardly, but they suffer from diseases because they do not have goodness in God's sight. They don't burst out in anger outwardly, but they keep the harmful ill-feelings, hatred, and resentment bottled up in their hearts. When we forgive and love others with a good heart that God wants, we can enjoy good health both in spirit and body.

Fourth, diseases sometimes come from the enemy devil and Satan

The result of the iniquity of idolatry, the worshiping of idols, is sin that is passed onto the children, even unto the third and the fourth generations (Exodus 20:5). The enemy devil and Satan bring afflictions and trials to the succeeding generations. That's why many families of idol-worshippers have sick, disabled, or demon-possessed members. The sins of their parents and ancestors have influences on their descendants. But even if parents worship idols, if the children are of goodness and worship God, He will protect them and give love and grace to them.

But some people are possessed by demons or evil spirits even though they have nothing to do with idols and do attend church. This is the case where though they sinned excessively though they say they believe and the accumulation of their evil crossed well beyond limits. But still, if such people thoroughly repent before God, He restores them and makes them whole.

Fifth, some problems are caused at one's stage of conception

Although their parents have no grave sins, some babies are born with deformities due to the combination of unhealthy egg and sperm.

However, most diseases or congenital diseases are caused when parents or ancestors worshipped idols excessively or piled up many sins. Therefore, I hope you will realize that the first priority is to solve the problem of sins and then to be healed. Resolve the problem of sin and enjoy good health both in spirit, mind and body.

Healing of Infirmities

God doesn't want His beloved children to suffer from diseases. So He sacrificed His only begotten Son to open the way of enjoying good health for us. By shedding His blood, Jesus redeemed us from all sins, and by His scourging we were healed (Isaiah 53:5; 1 Peter 2:24). Thus, anyone who believes it can be healed of diseases and even any kind of infirmities.

Infirmities, here, refer to conditions or problems of the body that cannot be cured with human ability or methods. It does not refer to minor ailments.

Infirmities refer to symptoms paralysis or degeneration of some body parts causing speech disorders, hearing-impairment, visual-impairment, walking disorder, or polio. We can be healed of various kinds of diseases when we repent of our sins, accept Jesus Christ, and receive the Holy Spirit. Even when we have serious diseases because we don't live according to God's Word in our Christian life, we can be healed by God by repenting of our sins and turning away from them.

Infirmities are only healed by the power of God. The prophets like Moses and Elijah in the Old Testament and the apostles Peter and Paul in the New Testament could heal infirmities because they received the power of God. To receive the power, we have to achieve whole sanctification and accumulate a myriad of prayers. Those who want to be healed should also have faith in Jesus Christ.

In Acts chapter 3, in the name of Jesus Christ, Peter raised up a lame man who begged alms at the gate of the Temple, and he stood up and walked. Because this beggar believed in Jesus Christ he could experience the amazing power of God. When we believe in Jesus Christ from the bottom of our hearts, we can experience amazing divine healing works.

"Lord, Help Me!"

Some fall as a result of their high self-esteem while others turn their misfortune into advantage by destroying such self-esteem. If you highly regard yourself in this way, you can't be first to offer your hand to a neighbor. You may even disregard your neighbor's helping hand or his plea. Due to inflated self-respect and self-esteem a small matter, that would otherwise be a trifle, could become so great that close friends become enemies on account of it.

Such high self-esteem benefits no one. A woman in the Bible received her answer by destroying her self-esteem.

When Jesus went to Syrophoenicia, a woman who had a demon-possessed daughter came to Him. She implored Him, *"Have mercy on me, Lord, Son of David; my daughter is cruelly demon-possessed. Lord, help me!"* (Matthew 15:22) Jesus answered and said, *"It is not good to take the children's bread and throw it to the dogs"* (v. 26). In other words, He likened the Israelites to the children, and the woman, who was a Gentile, to a dog.

Why did Jesus say such a thing? Ordinary people feeling such harsh treatment like this would probably feel quite offended and just leave. But, Jesus spoke this way to test the woman's faith in such a situation.

The woman was not disappointed. She didn't give up and did not allow her pride to interfere. She rather said, *"Yes, Lord; but even the dogs feed on the crumbs which fall from their masters' table"* (v. 27). What a wonderfully humble confession of faith this is!

Jesus was moved by her confession from her heart and said to her, *"O woman, your faith is great; it shall be done for you as you wish"* (v. 28). And her daughter was healed at once. When the woman humbled herself completely and implored without change, she was able to solve the problem of her daughter (Matthew 15:22-28). Like her case, God answers the prayer of those who destroy self-esteem and have a humble heart.

Destroy Wall of Sins

Among people who come to God, some seek Him out of their good conscience and others seek Him to resolve their problems. To solve problems in life, especially those of disease, they have to accept Jesus Christ and receive forgiveness of their sins first. As recorded in Isaiah 59:2, *"But your iniquities have made a separation between you and your God,"* they have to destroy the wall of sins against God. Then, what are these walls of sin that should be destroyed to solve problems?

First, we must repent not having believed in God and not having accepted Jesus Christ.

This is because John 16:8-9 reads, *"And He, when He comes, will convict the world concerning sin, and righteousness and judgment; concerning sin, because they do not believe in Me."* We can receive not only salvation, but also the keys to solve all the problems of our lives when we acknowledge God the Creator with humble hearts, and accept Jesus Christ, who was crucified to redeem us from sins, as our Savior.

Second, we have to repent that we don't love our brothers.

The Bible tells us that God's children should love not just one another, but even enemies. But if we hate our brethren instead of loving them it becomes a wall of sin before God because we violate His Word.

Third, we have to repent if we have prayed with greed.

James 4:2-3 says, *"... You do not have because you do not ask. You ask and do not receive, because you ask with wrong motives, so that you may spend it on your pleasures."* God isn't pleased when we pray to fulfill our greed or we ask to satisfy our personal pleasure. God also doesn't answer such prayers just as parents don't give allowance when their children ask for money to do something bad.

Fourth, we have to repent that we pray with doubt.

James 1:6-7 says that a person who has doubts in prayer should not expect that he will receive anything from the Lord. When we pray with doubts in our hearts, it shows that we don't believe God is the Almighty. So we need to repent of it and pray to have true faith.

Fifth, they have to repent that they didn't keep the commandments.

If we haven't done anything wrong in the light of God's Word, we can ask God with confidence and know that He answers our prayers (1 John 3:21-22). Therefore, if you want to receive answers, you should look back upon your life reflecting on the Ten Commandments which is a summary of the 66 books of the Bible. If you discover something in you that is in violation of the commandments, you have to turn away from it and keep the commandments.

Sixth, we have to repent that we didn't sow before God.

God lets us reap what we have sown. When we sow seeds of prayer, our souls prosper. When we sow seeds of voluntary service and deeds of faith, we become healthy in body and spirit. When we sow money, we can receive financial blessing.

Therefore, you have to repent if you wanted to receive answers without sowing. When we destroy the walls of sin and keep the Word, God is pleased and gives answers.

The Importance of Words from Lips

Some receive God's answers and blessings through positive words and professions of faith. But others don't receive answers due to their negative words although they work faithfully for God and pray diligently. In Matthew Chapter 8, Jesus praised a centurion's faith after He heard his confession and responded to him with an answer. What kind of confession did he make that he was able to receive a compliment and have his desire fulfilled by Jesus?

In Jesus' time, the Jews were subjugated and ruled by the Roman Empire. The Roman soldiers were stationed throughout Israel. Under such a situation and with such authority, it was not easy for a Roman centurion stationed in Israel to go to someone of the subjugated country and ask for something. But, the centurion possessed goodness, so without regard for his position of authority he went to Jesus with a humble heart. He implored Him to heal his servant saying, *"Lord, my servant is lying paralyzed at home, fearfully tormented"* (Matthew 8:6). Jesus saw his good heart and said, *"I will come and heal him"* (v. 7).

But the centurion made an unexpected confession to Him, *"Just say the word, and my servant will be healed"* (v. 8). He spoke the confession of faith saying that even though Jesus didn't go to his servant in person he knew that his servant would be healed by Jesus' Word. The reason he could say such a word of faith is that he believed for sure that Jesus was the Son of God. Then, Jesus praised him saying, *"I have not found such great faith with anyone in Israel"* (v. 10) and blessed him saying, *"Go, it shall be done for you as you have believed"* (v. 13). Then, his servant was healed that very moment.

The Bible puts an emphasis on words of our lips.

Psalm 34:12-13 says, *"Who is the man who desires life and loves length of days that he may see good? Keep your tongue from evil and your lips from speaking deceit."* Proverbs 13:2 reads, *"From the fruit of a man's mouth he enjoys good, but the desire of the treacherous is violence."* Through the passages, we can realize that we can receive blessing or face difficulties because of words from our lips.

Romans 10:10 also says, *"For with the heart a person*

believes, resulting in righteousness, and with the mouth he confesses, resulting in salvation." Jesus said in Matthew 10:32, *"Therefore everyone who confesses Me before men, I will also confess him before My Father who is in heaven."* These verses tell us that Christian faith is accompanied by the confession of faith. Therefore, I hope you will always enjoy a life full of answers and blessings through confessions of honesty and faith.

Throw Your Cloak Away

In our life journey, we come across problems both great and small. Some of them are impossible to solve with human power. But anyone who comes to the Lord can receive solutions to all their problems. Mark Chapter 10 talks about a man named Bartimaeus who was a blind beggar. If he had been able to see he would not have had to be a beggar. But due to his blindness there was nothing else for him but to beg. His life was so desperate. He wanted to see the world around him more than anything. One day, he met Jesus and his desire was fulfilled. Why was the blind Bartimaeus able to receive answers to his pleas?

First, because he had a good heart

Though Bartimaeus couldn't see, he still heard the amazing news that Jesus healed the sick and performed a number of signs and wonders. As faith grew in him his heart began to burn within him believing that his problem could also be solved if he could just meet Jesus. Bartimaeus had such a good heart that when he heard the gospel he was able to accept and believe what he heard.

Second, because he cried out in asking

After he heard that Jesus was going to come to the city of Jericho, he wanted to meet Jesus. The moment he had been waiting for finally came. Hearing what the people around him were saying, he knew that Jesus was approaching where he was sitting. He began to cry out, "Jesus, Son of David, have mercy on me!" Many people were sternly telling him to be quiet, but he kept crying out all the more, "Son of David, have mercy on me!" In Mark 10:46-52 we find that by his acts of faith, he received his answer. If we keep crying out in prayer with faith until the end and diligently seek Him, we can also receive answers from God (Jeremiah 29:12-13).

Third, because he threw his cloak away and came before Jesus

For a beggar his cloak is a very important possession. It is a necessity that he wears whether it's cold or hot. But Bartimaeus threw his cloak away, and jumped up and came to Jesus. Here, a cloak spiritually symbolizes filthy sin, and stench of an unclean heart. Thus, 'throwing his cloak' spiritually means the casting off of dishonesty, hatred, and greed in hearts and the act of repentance to come to a holy place.

Seeing Bartimaeus' faith and deed, Jesus said, "What do you want Me to do for you?" He said to Jesus, "I want to regain my sight!" and Jesus let him see as he wanted. Like him, when we cast off the stench and filthiness of sins and achieve a clean heart, we can meet the Lord and receive answers to any problem.

To Enjoy True Peace

People usually think that they can enjoy satisfaction and peace when they have many things. However, both the rich and the poor have their own worries in their life. If they don't know the right purpose and meaning of their life, they get worried about small matters. It leads them to have no true peace in them. Jesus said to them, *"Peace I leave with you; My peace I give to you; not as the world gives do I give to you. Do not let your heart be troubled, nor let it be fearful"* (John 14:27). Then, how can we enjoy true peace?

First, we should know our own duties and position.

Above all, we should clearly realize our duties and capabilities well. We can find our life worth living and enjoy true peace when we understand our position and fulfill our duties as parents, children, students or employees. In addition, when we do our best to fulfill our God-given duties as pastors, cell-group leaders, cell leaders, choir members, etc., joy and peace will come upon us. And when we measure our faith correctly and try to increase it to a higher level, God's grace will come upon us from above and we can fulfill our duties well.

Second, we should become the poor in spirit

The poor in spirit empty their hearts and feel satisfied with what they have now and do their best in their positions. They don't want to possess more than they ought to have since they have no greed. They live according to God's Word, not their own thoughts, so they don't have to suffer in their hearts and they enjoy true peace. On the contrary, the rich in spirit take in many things out of greed but they have no satisfaction, nor can they attain peace. That's why Ecclesiastes 1:8 says to us, *"All things are wearisome; man is not able to tell it. The eye is not satisfied with seeing, nor is the ear filled with hearing."*

Third, we should control our hearts and act in the truth.

Most people rejoice when something joyful happens, but they feel distressed and lose joy when something sad and sorrowful happens. But God tells us to rejoice always and give thanks in everything. God of love redeemed us from all our sins by sending His only begotten Son to this earth and gave us grace in which we can enjoy eternal life in the beautiful Heaven. Moreover, by sending the Helper the Holy Spirit to us, He let us live in the truth and achieve a victory all the time in God's help.

Those who realize God's love and grace try hard to act according to God's will and control their hearts under any circumstance. Because they have hope for Heaven, they can rejoice always and give thanks in everything. In doing so, God will give them true peace and answer their prayers quickly.

How to Beat Stress

Stress is spread among modern people widely enough to be called "the newly-discovered global epidemic." If you feel under stress, you feel worried and tense mentally and physically because of difficulties in your life. It is a major cause of various diseases. Then, how can cope with stress?

First, as individuals we must clearly understand the value and purpose of our lives

When we know the true value and purpose of our life with answers of the questions "Where did I come from, what do I live for, and where am I supposed to be going?" we don't have to feel worried about trivial matters and we are not concerned about them. Ecclesiastes 12:13 reads, *"The conclusion, when all has been heard, is: fear God and keep His commandments, because this applies to every person."*

Therefore, we should understand our duties as men and put hope in Heaven, and we must not be obsessed with the worldly matters. Then, we can live in joy and thanks without feeling stressed.

Second, we should commit everything to the Lord

Philippians 4:6-7 says, *"Be anxious for nothing, but in everything by prayer and supplication with thanksgiving let your requests be made known to God. And the peace of God, which surpasses all comprehension, will guard your hearts and your minds in Christ Jesus."* When you are faced with various problems, you should not be anxious, but instead pray committing everything to the Lord. Then the Lord will give you peace and cause everything to work together for good.

Third, we should take a rest on a regular basis

After creating the heavens and the earth and all things in them for six days, God rested on the seventh day. He also commanded us to work hard for six days and rest on the seventh day (Exodus 20:8-11). If we work diligently for six days and offer worship services to God in church on Sundays according to the Word of God, we can enjoy rest both in spirit and body. When we worship in spirit and truth during services we can make spiritual bread of God's Word, our souls enjoy prosperity, and tiredness in spirit and body go away.

Fourth, we should develop internal strength

As said in 1 John 4:4, *"You are from God, little children, and have overcome them; because greater is He who is in you than he who is in the world,"* God's children have the Helper the Holy Spirit in their hearts. The Holy Spirit gives us strength to pray, interceding for our weakness. He provides us with new strength (Romans 8:26). When we stay being filled with the Spirit by praying on the alert always, we can gain internal strength with which we can do everything and we can overcome any stressful situation. Therefore, I hope you will overcome all stress by faith in God and happiness and hope for Heaven will overflow in your heart.

Spiritual Law on Answers

God listens to our prayer, and gives answers according to the justice of the spiritual law. Such rules of justice are the seven Spirits of God.

Seven Spirits refer to the heart of God who is spirit. Here, "seven" doesn't mean that God has seven Spirits but means that God is perfect since "seven" is the number of perfectness. Seven Spirits search for hearts and deeds of men and work in accordance with justice for those who meet the required measures to receive answers. Thus, seven Spirits can be thought of as an instrument of measure or a scale of God to measure faith and give answers. Then, what is measured by the seven Spirits?

First is the measure of faith

God clearly says that it will be done as you believe. So if

we believe from heart and say something, it will be realized for sure. But if there is no answer, even if you profess your faith with your lips, your faith isn't the spiritual faith God acknowledges. Spiritual faith is given from God to the extent that we achieve sanctification. When we have such faith we can obey God's Word completely.

Second is the measure of joy

Before we believed in God we lived without true joy. But when we receive salvation and become people who are citizens of Heaven we cannot help but rejoice. It is because we realize we had once been on the way to Hell and eternal death, but we came to gain eternal life and become filled with hope for Heaven. That realization brings true joy springing up from the bottom of our hearts. Joy is a sign of God's children, and fragrance that sets apart men of Christ from others, and a proof that shows they have faith that can bring down answers. But if your love and passion cool down and your faith becomes lukewarm, or you commit sins and create walls of sin, joy will disappear. In such a case, we must recover the first love by destroying the walls of sin.

Third is the Seven Spirit's measure of prayer

We should pray in accordance with God's heart and will. The kind of prayer God wants is the prayer that is found in Luke 22:42-44. It is prayer acquired by habit and without ceasing. You also should kneel down in prayer and pray fervently according to God's will without seeking your own benefit. And, you should pray with faith and love. That is, you must pray with love for God believing God will give answers to you. God accepts the aroma of such prayer joyfully.

Fourth is the measure of thanks

Together with joy, thanksgiving is one of fruits that is evidence that we have become God's children. Those who believe God is alive and Heaven and Hell exist can give confessions of thanks all the time from the bottom of their hearts under any circumstances. God will cause all things to work together for the good when we give prayer of thanks with faith not only in favorable situation, but also in hardship.

Fifth is the seven Spirit's measure of keeping the commandments

Many passages in the Bible tell us to do, not to do, to keep, and to throw away something. The Ten Commandments summarizes the entire content of these laws and commandments.

Just as said in 1 John 5:3, *"For this is the love of God, that we keep His commandments,"* keeping the commandments is an evidence of love for God. Only when we show the love by keeping commandments, we can receive answers.

Sixth is the measure of faithfulness

The seven Spirits measure how faithfully we work before God when performing our duties. God wants us to work faithfully in all places—not only in church, but also in the family and workplace. God is pleased with spiritual faithfulness that is given with a holy heart free of evil.

Seventh is the measure of love

Love is like a cord that binds all the other six aspects together. It is the ultimate purpose for which we receive human cultivation on this earth. No matter what we do— whether praying or working faithfully—it's meaningful when we act with love for God and neighbors (1 Corinthians 13:1-3). Let's say, you seem to work faithfully to perform your duty, but you burst out in anger because of something that doesn't agree with your thoughts. Then, it means you did not fulfill your duty with love. When we cultivate love, we can say we have accomplished everything completely. We can then please

God and quickly receive answers, blessings and the healing of diseases.

God-pleasing Workers

"Let a man regard us in this manner,
as servants of Christ and stewards
of the mysteries of God. In this case,
moreover, it is required of stewards
that one be found trustworthy."

(1 Corinthians 4:1-2)

Those Who Have a Dream and Make It Come True

Those who have a dream are happy. As they set their plan in motion and try hard to accomplish it in order to make the dreams come true, their lives become more active and they feel happy. The greater their dream is, the greater the effort and patience they have to put into the plan and into making it happen. But after all the effort the fruit and joy they gain are incomparable with anything. Students have a dream to enter colleges or companies they want. And adults have a dream to possess their own homes or expand their businesses.

People have both small and big dreams in the way, and as God's children we should have dreams too. Our dreams are to gain eternal life by living a life that God wants; to be qualified to see the Lord by fulfilling our God-given duties; and saving as many souls as we can. By completely fulfilling these dreams believers will enjoy eternal glory and happiness in Heaven. How can we make such a dream come true?

First, we have to work faithfully

1 Corinthians 4:2 says, *"In this case, moreover, it is required of stewards that one be found trustworthy."* So we should work faithfully. Believers' duties are to worship in spirit and truth and to practice God's Word. Workers who are in charge of taking care of souls should take after new believers and those who have weak faith, help them grow up in spirit, and increase the number of the saved people day by day. To the extent that you work faithfully, heavenly rewards will be piled up and you will receive recognition and love from God and other church members.

Second, we must have spiritual plans

We should have spiritual plans to become better than now in faith. We should make plans to act according to Jesus' teaching. We must make spiritual bread of the Word of God and love and serve our brothers and sisters. Then, God will give necessary wisdom and lead you to the shortcut to making your dream come true.

Third, we should please God

Those who love God naturally love the church that is the

body of the Lord. They think "How can our church grow and give glory to God?" They also seek only God's kingdom and righteousness and try to please God in their faith. Hebrews 11:6 says, *"Without faith it is impossible to please Him, for he who comes to God must believe that He is and that He is a rewarder of those who seek Him."* So God is pleased with people who show perfect faith to God and He fulfills their hearts' desires.

Fourth, we must maintain patience in our perseverance

While you are trying to achieve a God-given dream, you might be faced with difficulties. Nevertheless, you should be patient, fulfill your duties, and keep and act within the Word of God. This course of action in faith is pleasing to God. When we act in God's will and ways, and receive His guidance, we can then achieve our dreams like Abraham and Joseph achieved theirs. So we also should have great dreams in the Lord, receive God's wisdom and strength, and greatly extend His kingdom.

Good Stewards

Those in the management level positions of companies want to hire people who can demonstrate outstanding talents. This is because it is the people who work for the company that decide the success or failure of the company. Likewise, God wants to choose people who are suitable for the purposes of His heart and He then entrusts them with tasks. So when we bear abundant fruit by following God's heart, He is pleased and acknowledges we are good stewards. Stewards in the Lord refer to people who manage the situations of the environment, finances, and time that God has given to them.

1 Peter 4:11 reads, *"Whoever speaks, is to do so as one who is speaking the utterances of God; whoever serves is to do so as one who is serving by the strength which God supplies; so that in all things God may be glorified through Jesus Christ, to whom belongs the glory and dominion*

forever and ever." Then, let's talk about what kind of people are good stewards God wants by examining five cases.

The first case is when the master falls into hardship or difficulties

Evil stewards avoid or turn their faces away from their master when the master encounters hardship. But good stewards take over the difficulty on the master's behalf even by sacrificing themselves. It is in this way that those who have a heart of serving their masters with their lives are good stewards.

The second case is in their service to their master

Evil stewards work only as much as they must do to keep from being reprimanded by their master. For example, some employees take frequent breaks, others are forced to do certain work only for the money, and still others work habitually with no joy or sense of value. But good stewards do everything with joy and thanks. They follow their master's will in all matters since they love their master from the bottom of their hearts. They handle all matters quickly by trying to understand the master's heart and intention and fill the master's shortcomings.

The third case is in the management of the master's finances

Evil stewards seek personal advantage and benefit by using what is the master's. On the other hand, good stewards increase what is entrusted to them by the master by working diligently. They do not have greed for anything, whether it is big or small. If we want to be a good steward for God's kingdom, we should give the tithe that is God's, and use the rest of money properly as well. You can't be good stewards if you don't give the tithe but use it for your benefit, or even if you give tithe but you use the nine tenths as you please thinking it is all yours, it is not being a good steward.

The fourth case is when they get promoted

Evil stewards get arrogant and look down on their master when they become skillful to some degree. But good stewards check themselves and serve their master with more humble hearts as they gain recognition. Good stewards of God's kingdom pray to fulfill their God-given duties, realize spiritual things, and obey. By doing so, they bear beautiful fruit.

The fifth case is when they meet with a situation that is extreme

Good stewards serve their master and work faithfully without change of heart whereas evil stewards will betray their master seeking their own benefit when they are faced with a life-or-death situation. Early church members willingly became prey for lions and were beheaded to keep their faith for the Lord. Such people are good stewards. And it is also the heart and deeds of good stewards to pray fervently for the kingdom of God, give fasting, and be devoted in all things.

Men Who Take Responsibility

Honest people don't change in any situation. They keep their word and their hearts, and they accept responsibility for their own deeds. They are able to lead the people around them on the right path, or they help out people who are in unfair situations by speaking honestly for them in their position. They naturally take responsibility for what they do or fail to do. They are trusted by their superiors who in turn entrust more important and greater tasks to them because they fulfill not only what is their part but also others'.

God's children should take responsibility like this for their own job, and they also should play the role of light and salt for all people. To do so what kinds of specific things do we need to do?

First, we should be an example demonstrating good words and deeds

Titus 1:7-9 says, *"For the overseer must be above reproach as God's steward...loving what is good, sensible, just, devout, self-controlled, holding fast the faithful word which is in accordance with the teaching..."* Therefore, workers who have God-given duties should keep in mind that the Lord has given them the duties for the church that He bought with His blood and be careful about all that you say and do. You also should sacrifice yourselves, work faithfully, and live an exemplary life for God's kingdom and righteousness with the heart of a good steward.

Second, we should preach the gospel and lead souls to the way of life

God desires all men to be saved and to come to the knowledge of the truth (1 Timothy 2:4). Thus, we must preach the gospel diligently to unbelievers with love, and plant faith in them, and increase the number of people who receive salvation. Just as the apostle Paul lectured to many souls and led them to the way of eternal life, we also must preach the gospel earnestly and lead them to live according to God's Words.

Third, we should have faith with which we long for the inheritance that God will give

Believers with true faith are faithful before God and devote themselves, but they rejoice without saying they are tired. This is because they have faith of seeing God who repays according to what they have done. The apostle Paul endured any sacrifice with joy because he saw inheritance God will give, namely, everlasting glory and rewards. He said in Philippians 2:17, *"But even if I am being poured out as a drink offering upon the sacrifice and service of your faith, I rejoice and share my joy with you all."*

A drink offering is a form of offering where people pour wine out upon the sacrifice. Then, the wine is smeared into the sacrifice and adds to the fragrance, but it isn't seen on the sacrifice. Just as the wine, the apostle Paul had a heart that would give everything even if he sacrificed himself and suffered from all kinds of difficulties. He would give without revealing his name as long as he could achieve God's kingdom and righteousness.

Fourth, we should care for one another

We should realize it is more blessed to give than to receive, provide church members with what they need, and try to serve visitors. We also should show good deeds and give alms to all people whenever we can, especially in the case of believers. By doing so, we can be the example demonstrating the service of the Lord. When we do good like this, God will most certainly cause our souls to prosper and make everything go well with us to the extent that we increase faith. How blessed it is that what we have sown on the earth will be piled up in Heaven as well as on this earth. Therefore, we must care for neighbors with faith and love and do good before God.

Righteous Men

People usually think of those who cannot tolerate unrighteousness and appear to have a strong sense of righteousness to be righteous men. But righteous men in God's sight are men who cast away sins and achieve righteousness in their hearts. Noah, who built the Ark in obedience to God; Zechariah and Elizabeth, who were the parents of John the Baptist; and Cornelius, the centurion, were recognized as being righteous by God. Then, what kind of heart and deeds characterize the righteous men God acknowledges?

First, they have good thoughts

Proverbs 11:23 says, *"The desire of the righteous is only good."* In reality, the righteous God acknowledges like Abraham, Joseph, and Daniel, even when they were faced with situations that were unfair, didn't think "How could this happen to me?" Instead they gave everything for others and quietly waited for God. They could always go the ways of prosperity because God dwelt with them and He saw their hearts and minds. Likewise, if we want to live a life of goodness, God will give us wisdom and let us take the prosperous way.

The second is they have borne the nine fruits of the Holy Spirit (Galatians 5:22-23)

Some people reveal evil and others show goodness in the very same situation, depending on what kind of hearts they have. To the extent that they posses hatred, jealousy, and greed, they tend to solve every problem in evil ways. On the contrary, those who have pure hearts with the fruits of love, joy, peace, patience, mercy, kindness, faithfulness, gentleness, and self-control deal with every problem in good ways.

Third, they seek others' benefits

The righteous men in God's sight don't seek their own benefits all the time. They don't cause problems for others but try to give joy and hope since they value everybody. They don't make careless mistakes, but they accept responsibility and help and encourage others to manage their duties and responsibilities. They can't commit sins before God. God loves such righteous men and stays with them in amazing love and grace.

Honest Men

Some people speak using righteous and good words all the time, while there are others who hurt others' feeling with evil words. Proverbs 16:13 says, *"Righteous lips are the delight of kings, and he who speaks right is loved."* Through this passage, we can understand that to have righteous lips we must speak right first, namely, speak honestly.

Here the term 'honest' is a relationship meaning that by keeping the Word of God in our hearts, God will present our hearts with the right way so that we can act according to it. Then, what kind of men are spiritually honest men?

First, Spiritually honest men acknowledge their mistakes and repent

God isn't pleased if we don't reveal our mistakes or faults fearing for reprimand. Such people don't spiritually grow up and have development in life. Spiritually honest men admit their faults honestly and know how to take responsibility and endure punishment that follows. Because they are honest and have a big vessel, they can change into men of the truth quickly.

Second, Spiritually honest men are able to discern between good and evil and choose goodness

Dishonest people seek their own benefits and choose evil when they have to choose between good and evil. Since they are obsessed with benefits before their eyes and reality, they could act in foolish ways. But we should take the right way although we are faced with difficulties. We have to choose goodness boldly by remembering Matthew 10:28 saying, *"Do not fear those who kill the body but are unable to kill the soul; but rather fear Him who is able to destroy both soul and body in hell."*

Third, spiritually honest men speak the truth even though they gain no benefit

Some people change their words or deny what they said fearing that they will meet with disadvantage by telling the truth. Also, some will leave a wrong that should be corrected without revealing the truth because they do not stand to gain the benefit or advantage. Some people tend to exaggerate things in excess of what is the truth as they think or feel. All of these situations are far from honesty and the character of a spiritually honest man. We can be honest men when we speak the truth even if there is no benefit.

People who Receive the Praise of the Lord

It is something very good to receive recognition and praise from people. This is because it is evidence that our hearts and deeds are seen to be edifying to our neighbors. Then, if we are praised and recognized by God, how great blessing it would be! In 2 Corinthians 10:18 we find written, *"For it is not he who commends himself that is approved, but he whom the Lord commends."* Then, I will talk about what kinds of men are praised by the Lord.

First, they will not point out the faults and shortcomings of others with evil intent

To receive the compliment of the Lord, you must not criticize others by passing judgment or condemnation on them with evil. You must not either ignore others or insist your opinion on others. You should not try to teach others all the time. Of course, if others ask you something or you are in the position of teaching others, you must give explanation so that they can realize things by themselves. But if you center your attention on others' shortcomings, it means that you don't respect them. So you should see others' strong points with a heart of serving.

Second, they do not burst out anger and cause torment to others

Even if a superior is a picky person who gets angry frequently, his subordinates should obey him in the will of God who respects the order. Meanwhile, superiors should take care of their subordinates with love and understanding. Proverbs 12:16 reads, *"A fool's anger is known at once, but a prudent man conceals dishonor."* James 1:20 says, *"For the anger of man does not achieve the righteousness of God."* You might think it is righteous for you to get angry, but your anger hurt others' feeling. Moreover, anger itself is far from God's righteousness.

Third, they don't sway no matter they get any compliments or reprimands

When they are complimented, narrow-minded people

tend to rejoice too much to control themselves. But the broad-minded look back on their deeds and check if they really do something worthy of the praise and rather behave and improve themselves. The narrow-minded lose strength in frustration when they are pointed out for their faults whereas broad-minded men give thanks and consider the incident as a reason to grow up. So the Lord praises those who have broad minds.

Fourth, they don't harbor hard-feelings

We have hard-feelings when we do not cast away the desire to be recognized and receive praise. Suppose others behave rudely to us. If we do not have fleshly minds, we might gently point out their impoliteness, but we will not have any hard-feelings. God told us to crucify the flesh with its passions and desires (Galatians 5:24), and He wants us to resemble the holy Lord by changing with the Word and prayer (1 Timothy 4:5; 1 Peter 1:16).

We Must Act Only in the Spirit

The works of God through the Holy Spirit have great power that moves people's hearts. They make people change and gain faith, without regard to how evil they are. Therefore, we should act in the works of the Holy Spirit all the time to change our hearts into good hearts and receive strength to save souls. The Holy Spirit who is the Spirit of God, searches all things, even the depths of God as written in 1 Corinthians 2:10, and leads us to the way of goodness. Then, what should we do to receive the works of the Holy Spirit?

First, we should follow the desire of the Spirit

Galatians 5:17 reads, *"For the flesh sets its desire against the Spirit, and the Spirit against the flesh; for these are in opposition to one another, so that you may not do the things that you please."* Before they completely change into men of spirit, God's children who have received the Spirit also have two hearts: the heart to follow the desire of the Holy Spirit and the heart to follow the desire of the flesh.

The Spirit leads us to the truth and the way of salvation. On the other hand, the desire of the flesh guides us to sin, unrighteousness, and lawlessness, and triggers conflicts and makes people receive the works of Satan so that they can't work for the Holy Spirit. To the extent that our faith increases and we become men of spirit, we can curtail the heart of following the desire of the flesh and follow the desire of the Spirit more. Then, we can bear abundant fruit of the Holy Spirit.

Second, we should long for the works of the Holy Spirit

When we receive the Holy Spirit, we become men who always praise and pray. We come to wait for Sunday and long to listen to the Word of God and diligently gather in the sanctuary. Then, we naturally live according to God's will. In addition, if we want to receive God's grace and strength, we should long for the works manifested by the Holy Spirit.

Let's suppose a church worker prays for a sick person, and she is healed. Then, those who long for the works of the Holy Spirit don't think that she alone can manifest such a work. They pray more earnestly wanting to receive such strength so that they also can manifest the works of the Spirit. God is pleased with people who try to achieve those good works and He adds more strength to them.

Third, we should hear the voice of the Holy Spirit and obey His voice

Those who hear and obey the voice of the Spirit make no mistake because the Spirit clearly teaches them where to go and what to do. In order to hear the voice of the Holy Spirit, we should arm ourselves with the Word of God. Then, the Spirit makes His voice heard in our hearts with the Word of God which is the truth. And when we pray fervently, our fleshly thoughts are demolished. Then we can hear His voice more clearly and obey Him.

Fourth, we should receive the guidance of the Holy Spirit

The apostle Paul, who preached the message to the Gentiles, decided to go to Asia before he headed on the second missionary journey because his hometown was in Asia and he had already preached in Asia before. However, the Spirit of Jesus forbade him to speak the word in Asia, and God showed him vision that a man of Macedonia was standing and appealing to him, and saying, "Come over to Macedonia and help us." So he changed his plan, and headed for Macedonia because he realized that it was God's will for him to do his ministry in Macedonia (Acts 16:6-10). When we hear the voice of the Holy Spirit and obey Him, we can receive the guidance of the Spirit like this.

Fifth, we should speak with utterance given by the Holy Spirit

After the Lord ascended into Heaven, Peter received the Holy Spirit, healed men born with disabilities and preached the gospel before many people. When Peter preached the message in the portico of Solomon, the number of men who accepted the Lord through his sermons reached approximately 5,000 (Acts Chapters 1-4). At first, people thought Peter as an ordinary fisherman. But they were amazed by his sermon because he preached by the inspiration of the Holy Spirit. Therefore, I hope you will follow the example of such forefathers of faith, receive the works of the Holy Spirit, bear abundant fruit, and give glory to God.

To Bear Abundant Fruit

John Chapter 15 likens Jesus to the vine, and Christians to its branch. Just as branches can be provided with nutrients and bear fruit when they are attached to the vine, we also can bear abundant fruit only when we become united with the Lord. Then, what do we have to do in order to bear abundant fruit in the Lord and give glory to God?

First, we should pray fervently and fast

This is likened to cultivating a field to turn it into good soil and giving fertilizer to let the grain grow well. If we plant the Word of God in us, we should bear abundant good fruit by cultivating our heart-fields with fervent prayer and fasting. Even though we have faith that is as small as a mustard seed, we can increase our faith and receive God's strength, if we pray fervently and offer fasting.

Second, we should be resolute in casting away sin and evil

When growing grapes, nobody just leaves spoiled grapes on the vine because the rotten grapes will cause other fresh grapes to rot. Sins are the same. No matter how small they are, they grow into bigger sins when we just leave them be (Galatians 5:9). Therefore, we should cast them away quickly when we discover sins and evil like hatred, jealousy, anger, judgment, and an adulterous mind. God searches His children all the time for them so as not to commit sins and go to the way of death, and reprimands or refines them when they have wrongdoings. Through this process, He wants us to realize our sins and change.

Third, we should put our root of faith deep down

There are many steps until trees grow up well and bear fruit. They sometimes have to endure floods, droughts, and abnormal climate changes. Tress that put their roots deep down in the ground don't fall in heavy rains and strong winds, and they are even provided with water during drought and bear good fruit. Meanwhile, trees that don't have roots deep in the ground collapse due to rain, topple in strong wind and dry up when drought can't be endured.

To bear beautiful fruit in our Christian lives we should take deep root in faith. To do so, we should run in the fullness of the Holy Spirit and stand firmly on the Word of God. Those who stand on the rock of faith discern in the truth all the time, so they don't fall into the world and they are not tempted by the world. If we pray fervently, cast away sins, fill our shortcomings by checking in the light of the truth, we can bear abundant fruit.

Peace with All Men

A lot of problems take place when peace is broken among people. Discord in family takes away love and happiness, and conflicts among coworkers serve as a stumbling stone for the development of the company. So it is very important to have peace in our lives. In addition, Hebrews 12:14 reads, *"Pursue peace with all men, and the sanctification without which no one will see the Lord."* So we should keep peace if we love the Lord. Then, what should we do to keep peace with all men?

First, we should follow righteousness according to the order

If a subordinate reveals the king's fault and embarrasses him in front of many people, what would happen? Even if he does so out of good intention, it's not right because it causes troubles to the king. The same applies in families, workplaces, and among neighbors. We have to act in goodness and the truth in obedience of God's words telling us to do, not to do, to keep, and to throw away something, while following the order without embarrassing others. Then, we can say that we act in the truth and righteousness.

Second, we should not become enemies with anybody

During the Joseon (Choson) Dynasty, Jo Gwang-jo, who was an upright and righteous man, initiated sweeping reform. But he was sentenced to death due to opposing party's evil scheme because he had unconditionally ostracized the opponents. If he had embraced them wisely, he would have achieved great success in the reformation. Meanwhile, Jesus didn't say anything that could be found to be flawed, and in practicing righteousness all situations and circumstances were controlled without being spoken. In our following of Jesus we should not cause enmity with anyone. We must make our words and deeds perfect.

Third, we should not ignore others

If a person thinks they know about something more than someone else, in general they talk to them in the same manner as if they were teaching them. Even if they don't intend to ignore the listeners, the listener might feel they are ignored. Therefore, we have to get rid of the attitude of teaching and explain things so that they can understand well and deal with everything with a humble heart. Then, you can have peace with anybody.

To Become United in the Lord

Our body has many members, and we can keep in good shape when they fulfill their duties and become united as one. Likewise, we as a member of the church that is the body of Christ, we can give glory to God when we are united as one. Then, what can we do to become united as one in the Lord?

First, we should work with all our hearts

Those who work with all their hearts don't avoid reality even if it is very harsh and difficult to swallow. They don't change following their own benefits, but follow their duties until the end. This is because they have the heart of serving the Lord all the time with hearts and devotion (Colossians 3:23). These people always think "How can I work better and give glory to God?" so they joyfully do things that other don't want to do.

Second, we should work with all our souls

Early church members and the Lord's disciples preached the gospel without fear of death and kept their faith because they became united as one in their love for God. With their faith and devotion, the gospel was preached not only in the Roman Empire but also in the whole world. When we have such a heart of giving up our life for right things, we can overcome any hardship and give glory to God.

Third, we should work with all our minds

Jesus said to us, *"You shall love the Lord your God with all your heart, and with all your soul, and with all your mind"* (Matthew 22:37). "With minds" means that we deny ourselves according to God's will, not use human thoughts. For example, we have to have a heart of giving up a way even if your thought and way look better than any other ideas to succeed. In the way, when we demolish our own thoughts and follow God's will, we can become united as one.

Dwelling Place and Rewards Given As We Act

The God of justice repays what we have done and lets us reap what we have sown (2 Corinthians 9:6). Revelation 22:12 reads, *"Behold, I am coming quickly, and My reward is with Me, to render to every man according to what he has done."* And Revelation 2:23 states, *"...and I will give to each one of you according to your deeds."* Thus, it's important to receive salvation and enter Heaven, but it's also very important which dwelling place we will enter and what kinds of rewards we will receive. Then, how will dwelling places and rewards be decided in Heaven?

First of all, each person's heavenly dwelling place is different according to how prosperous each soul is by having kept God's commandments with love for Him.

Depending on how much you strive against sins even to

the point of shedding blood and how much you become sanctified, some of you will go to Paradise and some of you will go to the most glorious place in Heaven, New Jerusalem.

Next, heavenly rewards will be different according to how many souls we lead to the arms of God and how sincerely we give offerings to God.

The materials for our heavenly homes will be determined by the extent to which we endeavor to save souls on the earth and our works to achieve the many things of God's kingdom through our offerings, our deeds, and our efforts. It is in this way that our home's size and the degree of the beauty are determined. All things with which we give glory to God while on the earth will turn out to be rewards. These rewards will become accessories and ornaments in our homes. The light of glory will be different from person to person. The attire, patterns of the attire, accessories, hair style, and crowns received will be different as well. This is how we will be able to tell the level of sanctification that was achieved from person to person and how faithful they were on the earth.

Through this, we understand how much God is pleased with righteous men, loves those who have no evil, and how much He delights in our preaching the gospel with our love for the souls. Always live in the Word and bear abundant fruit of evangelization so that you will have glorious heavenly dwelling places and rewards in Heaven.

One Who Serves is Great

People who live by the law of the jungle cannot enjoy peace in their hearts and they are always nervous. Today, there are so many people who exert lawlessness and unrighteousness with greed to become greater than others even by trampling on them. But, when people possess fame, authority, honor, and glory in this way, all things will be revealed whether they are of goodness or of evil and they will suffer from difficulties that follow.

Even if they have such things before death, they can't take any of them when they leave this life. How meaningless it is! Thus, we must not work for meaningless and temporary things, but we must work for true and eternal things and become great men in Heaven.

Then, how can we become a great man in the Lord?

Matthew 20:26-28 says, *"It is not this way among you, but*

whoever wishes to become great among you shall be your servant, and whoever wishes to be first among you shall be your slave; just as the Son of Man did not come to be served, but to serve, and to give His life a ransom for many." Jesus is the Son of God and has everything, but He came to the earth in the form of man and served all men. So God exalted Him, and made Him the King of kings and the Lord of lords. (Revelation 17:14)

The day before His crucifixion, He washed His disciples' feet and showed them an example of humbleness and service. He taught them saying in John 13:14, *"If I then, the Lord and the Teacher, washed your feet, you also ought to wash one another's feet."* In other words, He taught them that they could become great men in Heaven when they served others in the truth just as Jesus humbled Himself and washed their feet. We should serve others from the bottom of their hearts since great men on the earth are great only temporarily, but great men of Heaven are great forever.

Excellent Man, Blessed Man

"Now it shall be, if you diligently obey
the LORD your God, being careful to
do all His commandments
which I command you today,
the LORD your God will set you high
above all the nations of the earth.
All these blessings will come upon you
and overtake you if you obey
the LORD your God."

(Deuteronomy 28:1-2)

Noah, Blameless Man in His Time

Noah was a righteous man, blameless in his time. He was saved even when all people of the world stained with sins fell in the judgment (Genesis Chapter 6). Seeing his righteousness, God let him know the upcoming judgment of water and guided him to prepare the ark. In the same way, when we become righteous men like Noah, God guides us to prosperous ways in any circumstances. Then, what should we do to become a blameless man like Noah?

First, we should long for the Word of God.

1 Peter 2:1-2 reads, *"Therefore, putting aside all malice and all deceit and hypocrisy and envy and all slander, like newborn babies, long for the pure milk of the word."* The 'pure milk of the word' refers to God's Word. Therefore, longing for the pure milk of the Word is to learn the will of

God, pay attention to His Word, live in goodness and get rid of every form of evil.

Second, we should have perfect hearts that are not stained with the worldly temptation.

Most of things in the world are meaningless and vain, so we must not be swept by the temptations of the world. To do so, we should gather in the sanctuary continually and break bread of the Word like Early Church members. We also should take care of one another, give alms to the poor, take care of orphans and widows, and act in goodness.

Third, we should be partakers of the divine nature (2 Peter 1:4)

To take part in the divine nature means that we become holy and perfect by casting away sins and evil from our hearts just as God is holy and perfect. God said in Leviticus 11:45, *"You shall be holy, for I am holy."* Jesus also said in Matthew 5:48, *"Therefore you are to be perfect, as your heavenly Father is perfect."* When we become righteous men God acknowledges by obeying God's Words and changing into holy and perfect men, we will be guided by God and everything will be prosperous and we will greatly achieve God's will.

Abraham,
Who Received Blessings

Abraham, the forefather of faith received the blessing of Jehovah-jireh. Jehovah-jireh is one of God's names that means 'God who provides beforehand'. The name is touching enough to move our hearts greatly. Then, what kind of faith did Abraham possess to receive such blessings?

First, he loved God more than anything else

Abraham was truthful and he had no deceitfulness. He was an upright and honest man. If it was God's will he could obey whatever God asked. When God said to him, *"Go forth from your country, and from your relatives and from your father's house, to the land which I will show you,"* he obeyed (Genesis 12:1-4). The attitude to obey every will of God is a proof that we love God more than anything else.

Second, he pursued peace with all men and sought sanctification

Abraham had a heart that pursued peace with all men. It was with love and care that he let his nephew, Lot, choose the better land to settle on and live. And he didn't want anything if it was not his because he pursued sanctification. When Lot was captured by other kings, Abraham went there to save him. But he didn't take away any spoils of the war at all. He also turned down the favor of Heth and paid proper price when he bought his wife's burial site. He had such a pure heart with no selfish-motives.

Third, he believed the power of God the Creator

When God told him to offer up Isaac as a burnt offering like an animal, he obeyed, even in a situation that was impossible to obey with human thoughts, because he believed God's promise concerning Isaac and the power of God who can revive the dead (Genesis 22:1-10). God considered his obedience and faith as righteousness, so He prepared a ram for the burnt offering and revealed Himself as Jehovah-jireh. He also blessed Abraham to become a blessing as the forefather of faith.

Joseph, Prosperous Man in Everything

Joseph was the eleventh son of Jacob. He was sold as a slave to Egypt by his brothers, but he became a ruler of all the Egypt after the Pharaoh and saved Egypt, his family, and himself during severe famine. We will talk about how he could receive recognition from others and give glory to God in such desperate circumstances and conditions and what kind of faith he had.

First, Joseph was a man who God was with.

Genesis 39:3 reads, *"Now his master saw that the LORD was with him."* Joseph became a slave regardless of his will, but he didn't feel frustrated about his situation. He just relied on God and practiced God's Word. His deeds and his heart were right and proper in God's sight, so God was with him and gave him the blessing of all things going well.

If God is with us, nothing matters, even if we fall into difficult situations. Anyone who completely relies on God and acts according to the Word of God can receive blessing of prosperity in everything because God is with him or her.

Second, Joseph was a diligent man

Joseph did his best with given conditions and worked diligently and faithfully. When he was sold in Egypt to Potiphar, he did his best to work for his master. He obeyed and worked diligently. He did the same when he was imprisoned due to wrongful accusation. He was also diligent there, so the chief jailer committed all the prisoners who were in the jail to Joseph's charge. The chief jailer even didn't supervise anything under Joseph's charge (Genesis 39:22-23). We can also be recognized by those around us and glorify God when we try our best to fulfill our duties wherever we might be—in our workplace, in school, and in the family.

Third, Joseph didn't cross the line and go beyond his limits or boundaries

Since Joseph was handsome in form and appearance, Potiphar's wife often tempted him to lie with her. He rejected every time, and didn't commit sins but said to her, *"How then could I do this great evil and sin against God?"* (Genesis 39:9) Then, when the appointed time came, God set him as a ruler of Egypt after the Pharaoh. By following his faith, we must not compromise with unrighteousness and do evil by being enticed by temptation or greed or seeking our own benefit. We must always walk the right path.

Moses, Faithful in All God's Household

Faithfulness is to perform our duties with all our hearts, minds, dedication, and life. God gave Moses who was faithful with special love saying, *"Not so, with My servant Moses, he is faithful in all My household; with him I speak mouth to mouth, even openly, and not in dark sayings, and he beholds the form of the LORD"* (Numbers 12:7-8). What were Moses' characters by which he could receive such love and blessing of God?

First, he loved God and his people to the utmost degree

Moses was born when Egypt severely persecuted the Israelites. Since they increased greatly and multiplied in number, the Pharaoh of Egypt was afraid of them and issued a command to kill the new-born sons when the Hebrew women gave birth. So Moses was destined to be put to death because he was among those sons. But his parents hid him for three months. When she could hide him no longer, she got a wicker basket and put the child into it and set it among the reeds by the bank of the Nile. The basket was spotted by Pharaoh's daughter and she took Moses as her son. Then, she met Miriam who was Moses' sister. Miriam recommended her mother who was Moses' biological mother to be his nurse. So Moses was able to learn about God and his people through his biological mother.

One day, Moses killed an Egyptian he saw beating an Israelite. He had to flee from the palace on account of this incident. He then started a life in wilderness (Exodus 2:11-15). If he had cared about his own position and happiness, he would have been indifferent about his people's sufferings. However, he couldn't just watch the sufferings of his people because he chose to endure ill-treatment with the people of God than to enjoy the passing pleasures of sin. He took the way of suffering because he loved God and his people and valued eternal rewards in Heaven more than all kinds of jewels in Egypt (Hebrews 11:26).

Second, he was very humble more than any man who was on the face of the earth.

During the journey to the land of Canaan, Moses had many difficulties as the leader of the sons of Israel. They complained and bore grudges against him whenever they were faced with difficult situations although they had seen God's signs and wonders. They even wanted to stone Moses. What's worse, they made a calf of molten gold and worshipped saying it was their god while Moses was on the mountain receiving the Ten Commandments. Seeing them, God decided to destroy them and made a great nation with Moses' descendants. Then, Moses gave a prayer of love to God, *"But now, if You will, forgive their sin—and if not, please blot me out from Your book which You have written!"* (Exodus 32:32) Because he earnestly wanted to save the people of Israel out of his gentleness, God acknowledged him as a humble man saying, *"He is very humble more than any man who was on the face of the earth"* (Numbers 12:3).

Third, he was faithful in all God's household

Just as said above, faithfulness is to perform our duties with all our hearts, minds, dedication, and life. When you are faithful in all aspects of your life such as in the workplace, school, and church, you can say you are faithful in all God's household.

Though Moses was the leader of a nation, he was a humble

man enough to pay heed to the advice of his father-in-law, Jethro (Exodus 18:13-26). And he prayed for his sister, Miriam, when she came down with leprosy because she bore a grudge against Moses. She was healed through Moses' prayer (Numbers 12:9-16). The Israelites complained and bore grudges against him countless times, but he kept patient with love and led them diligently. Hebrews 3:5 says, *"Now Moses was faithful in all His house as a servant, for a testimony of those things which were to be spoken later."* A servant refers to a worker who is employed for small things, so we can know how much Moses humbled himself and how faithful he was.

David, a Man after the Heart of God

David was the youngest among Jesse's eight sons and he was a shepherd. One day, Samuel the prophet came to Jesse's house by God's instruction. Samuel paid attention to Eliab who had outstanding appearance at first but God had him anoint David as the king, saying, *"Man looks at the outward appearance, but the LORD looks at the heart"* (1 Samuel 16:7). David was told by God he was a man after the heart of God. What kind of man was he so that he could receive such love and blessing?

First, he was a man who feared God.

Proverbs 8:13 reads, *"The fear of the LORD is to hate evil."* Since David revered and loved God, he led a God-pleasing life by leaving evilness and keeping the Word of God (Psalm 119:74). He once took Bathsheba from her husband, Uriah, and arranged for him to be killed by Gentiles on the battle field. But, he immediately repented when Nathan the prophet rebuked him.

Second, he fulfilled his duty even with his life

His confession makes us know his heart when he as a boy shepherded his father's flock. 1 Samuel 17:34-35 says, *"When a lion or a bear came and took a lamb from the flock, I went out after him and attacked him, and rescued it from his mouth; and when he rose up against me, I seized him by his beard and struck him and killed him."* As he said, he guarded the flock assigned to him with his life.

Third, he had true faith

Goliath was a Philistine giant of about three meters (9'9") in height. He wore a bronze helmet, scaled armor and carried a bronze javelin. David was a boy who went to the battlefield to run an errand for his father while shepherding the flock. But he couldn't stand it when Goliath insulted the army of the living God day and night for 40 days. Unarmed, he boldly came to Goliath just with a sling and stones. This is because he had true faith with which he relied on God the Almighty. He could achieve the stunning victory because he believed from the heart that God was always with him and guided him in prosperous ways. When he slung the stone, it struck Goliath's forehead and the war turned into the Israel's favor (1 Samuel 17:46-49).

Fourth, he did good until the end

King Saul set David over the men of war because he was wise and brave. When David returned with victory from the battle field, there were women who were singing, *"Saul has slain his thousands, and David his ten thousands"* (1 Samuel 18:7). Saul became jealous of David. He even hurled his spear at David to kill him while he was playing the harp for him who suffered from an evil spirit. But David didn't kill King Saul even when he had chances to kill King Saul. David pursued only goodness whereas King Saul made many attempts to kill David.

Even if people have three attributes explained above, if they have hearts that change for personal benefit, they can be perfect vessels. But if you unchangingly act in goodness and walk the right path, you can become one of the precious ones who receive God's love like David received.

Daniel Who Received God's Grace

Many people do not enjoy true peace due to many kinds of problems that arise in the world. But the Bible tells us that those who have sincere faith have nothing to worry about. Daniel was seized as a captive but became a commissioner and lived a life of only giving glory to God. Then, what kind of faith did Daniel have and how could he receive God's grace?

First, he showed firm love towards God

Daniel was taken captive when Nebuchadnezzar was the King of Babylon and invaded Southern Judah. The King of Babylon brought the most intelligent youths among captives and taught them the literature and language for three years. They even ate the king's choice food. Daniel was one of them. He sought permission from the chief of the officials not to be given the king's choice food. He feared that the food might contain the things sacrificed to idols or abominable food. In this way, he showed his love and reverence for God and tried to keep His commandments. So, in return, God controlled all situations around him and caused all things to work together for the good. In addition, He gave him the ability to understand all kinds of visions and dreams. When we clearly show love for God under any situation, we can receive love and grace from Him.

Second, he kept faith in God without changing

Other commissioners tried to wrongfully accuse Daniel out of jealousy because he received the love of Darius the King of Babylon as the commissioner. They asked the king to establish an injunction. They said the king should establish an injunction that anyone who made a petition to any god or man besides the king for 30 days shall be cast into the lions' den. Daniel knew about it, but he prayed with the windows open towards Jerusalem three times a day as usual. In the end, he was cast into the den in accusation of violating the injunction but God sent His angel and shut the lions' mouths and they didn't harm him.

Daniel knew all things that he had were given by God's grace, so he didn't compromise but kept faith even in danger of death. Like this, if we walk the right path without compromising with the world, God will protect and guard us.

Third, he tried to perform duties and work faithfully

He worked diligently and faithfully as the Chief Prefect over all the wise men of Babylon in the time of King Nebuchadnezzar, and he was one of the three commissioners in Persia in the time of King Darius. To Daniel who was earnest and faithful in everything, God showed in the visions what would happen in the future in the world (Daniel chapter 9). Like Daniel, we also should please to God with deeds of sincere faith and receive God's grace and love.

Mary Magdalene Who Anointed with Perfume

In His public ministry Jesus healed the sick, preached the gospel of Heaven, and gave hope and comfort to many people. Mary Magdalene grew up in the area where idol-worshipping was rampant from generation to generation, so she was suffering from all kinds of diseases under the forces of darkness. In the meantime, she heard about Jesus and came to have faith that she could be healed of her weakness and diseases if she met Him.

She finally heard that Jesus came to her town, and she came to Jesus with an alabaster vial of perfume. She couldn't dare stand before Him, so she stood behind Him at His feet, weeping. She began to wet His feet with her tears and kept wiping them with the hair of her head, and anointing them with the valuable perfume after breaking the vial.

Since Mary Magdalene came before Jesus and showed her heart with faith, she was forgiven of her sins by the grace of

God and received healing of all her diseases as well as salvation.

Then, what does Mary Magdalene breaking the alabaster vial and anointing Jesus' feet with perfume spiritually symbolize?

Here, 'an alabaster vial' spiritually symbolizes a body. To break an alabaster vial means to dedicate oneself to Jesus by giving his or her body. No matter how expensive perfume is, we can pour the perfume only after breaking the vial. In other words, dedication is accomplished only when we give up ourselves completely without considering our authority or position. Otherwise, we can't completely dedicate ourselves because of our thinking, "What will other people think of this?"

At that time perfume was very expensive. Therefore, Mary Magdalene's breaking the vial and anointing Jesus with the perfume spiritually means that she gave all her heart and mind to Him. As she washed Jesus' feet with her hair it showed the depth and sincerity of her humble heart, her service, her earnest love, and her devotion. We also should break all fleshly things like pride and arrogance and give the most valuable heart and devotion to the Lord.

The Apostle Paul
with Unchanging Faith

The apostle Paul had been zealous for Judaism, and took the lead in putting those who believed Jesus Christ behind bars and killing them. But he was converted after he met the Lord, and afterwards he preached the gospel to countless people as an apostle of Gentile men and established churches. He ran the way of faith with an unchanging heart under any persecution (Acts 20:24).

There was a time when he was beaten and imprisoned for his preaching the gospel, he only prayed and praised God. Then, suddenly there came a great earthquake, so that the foundations of the prison were shaken and all the doors were opened (Acts 16:25-26). Also, when he was in the prison of Philippi, he didn't get frustrated or sorrowful, but rather advised the members of Philippi Church to rejoice always (Philippians 4:4).

He didn't say he was distressed and he never denied Jesus

Christ even when he was in danger of death and he was cut off from all hope of living (2 Corinthians 1:8, 11:23). He always rejoiced, gave thanks, and worked faithfully just because of his hope for Heaven.

So the apostle Paul said in 2 Timothy 4:7-8, *"I have fought the good fight, I have finished the course, I have kept the faith; in the future there is laid up for me the crown of righteousness, which the Lord, the righteous Judge, will award to me on that day; and not only to me, but also to all who have loved His appearing."*

God is looking for those who have unchanging faith like the apostle Paul, and achieves His works and receives glory through them.

But some people complain after working faithfully for God. It means that they don't work with faith, so God is not pleased with their deeds, no matter how hard they work. This is because God joyfully accepts only what we do with faith. We should work for God's kingdom with unchanging faith, hope for Heaven, and thanks like the apostle Paul did.

Excellent Man, Blessed Man

There are many people in the world who have made great contribution in their individual fields. Their conviction was steady, and they set a specific goal and didn't spare their lives to achieve it. So they could leave their footprint in history. But we cannot say that they were excellent men if their achievement ended in this world. We can say those who shed light of the truth on the world were truly excellent men.

Then, what should we do in order to enjoy a valuable life as a truly excellent and blessed man?

Deuteronomy 28:1 reads, *"Now it shall be, if you diligently obey the LORD your God, being careful to do all His commandments which I command you today, the LORD your God will set you high above all the nations of the earth."* To become an excellent man, we should live a holy life by living by all God's commandments and following His will perfectly.

The God of love wants us to become not only an excellent man but also a blessed man. Deuteronomy 28:2-6 says, *"All these blessings will come upon you and overtake you if you obey the LORD your God... Blessed shall you be when you come in, and blessed shall you be when you go out."* Here, 'to obey' means that not just doing what we can do with our own strength, but also obeying with faith the commands of God that cannot be understood with human knowledge and experience or that seem impossible to be carried out with human ability.

The biblical forefathers of faith like Daniel, Joseph, Abraham, and Moses joyfully obeyed God as explained above. They believed God, kept all His commandments, and rejoiced and gave thanks under any circumstances and conditions. They eventually became blessed men, achieved great things of God, and gave glory to God. We also can such excellent and blessed men like the forefathers of faith when we pay attention to the Word of God and obey it.

The Author
Dr. Jaerock Lee

Dr. Jaerock Lee was born in Muan, Jeonnam Province, Republic of Korea, in 1943. In his twenties, Dr. Lee suffered from a variety of incurable diseases for seven years and awaited death with no hope for recovery. One day in the spring of 1974, however, he was led to a church by his sister and when he knelt down to pray, the living God immediately healed him of all his diseases.

From the moment Dr. Lee met the living God through that wonderful experience, he has loved God with all his heart and sincerity, and in 1978 he was called to be a servant of God. He prayed fervently with countless fasting prayers so that he could clearly understand the will of God, wholly accomplish it and obey the Word of God. In 1982, he founded Manmin Central Church in Seoul, Korea, and countless works of God, including miraculous healings, signs and wonders, have been taking place at his church.

In 1986, Dr. Lee was ordained as a pastor at the Annual Assembly of Jesus' Sungkyul Church of Korea, and four years later in 1990, his sermons began to be broadcast in Australia, Russia, the Philippines, and many more through the Far East Broadcasting Company, the Asia Broadcast Station, and the Washington Christian Radio System.

Three years later in 1993, Manmin Central Church was selected as one of the "World's Top 50 Churches" by the Christian World magazine (US) and he received an Honorary Doctorate of Divinity from Christian Faith College, Florida, USA, and in 1996 a Ph. D. in Ministry from Kingsway Theological Seminary, Iowa, USA.

Since 1993, Dr. Lee has been spearheading world evangelization through many overseas crusades in Tanzania, Argentina, L.A., Baltimore City, Hawaii, and New York City of the USA, Uganda, Japan, Pakistan, Kenya, the Philippines, Honduras, India, Russia, Germany, Peru, Democratic Republic of the Congo, Israel and Estonia.

In 2002 he was called a "worldwide revivalist" by major Christian newspapers in Korea for his powerful ministries in various overseas crusades. Especially, his

'New York Crusade 2006' held in Madison Square Garden, the most world-famous arena, was broadcast to 220 nations, and in his 'Israel United Crusade 2009' held in International Convention Center in Jerusalem he boldly proclaimed Jesus Christ is the Messiah and Savior. His sermon is brodacst to 176 nations via satellites including GCN TV and he was listed as one of the Top 10 Most Influential Christian Leaders of 2009 and 2010 by the Russian popular Christian magazine *In Victory* and new agency *Christian Telegraph* for his powerful TV broadcasting ministry and overseas church-pastoring ministry.

As of August of 2013, Manmin Central Church has a congregation of more than 120,000 members. There are 10,000 branch churches throughout the globe including 56 domestic branch churches, and so far more than 123 missionaries have been commissioned to 23 countries, including the United States, Russia, Germany, Canada, Japan, China, France, India, Kenya, and many more.

As of the date of this publishing, Dr. Lee has written 87 books, including bestsellers *Tasting Eternal Life before Death, My Life My Faith I & II, The Message of the Cross, The Measure of Faith, Heaven I & II, Hell, Awaken Israel,* and *The Power of God.* His works have been translated into more than 76 languages.

His Christian columns appear on *The Hankook Ilbo, The Chosun Ilbo, The JoongAng Daily, The Dong-A Ilbo, The Munhwa Ilbo, The Seoul Shinmun, The Kyunghyang Shinmun, The Korea Economic Daily, The Korea Herald, The Shisa News, and The Christian Press.*

Dr. Lee is currently leader of many missionary organizations and associations: including Chairman, The United Holiness Church of Jesus Christ; President, Manmin World Mission; Permanent President, The World Christianity Revival Mission Association; Founder & Board Chairman, Global Christian Network (GCN); Founder & Board Chairman, World Christian Doctors Network (WCDN); and Founder & Board Chairman, Manmin International Seminary (MIS).

Heaven I & II

A detailed sketch of the gorgeous living environment the heavenly citizens enjoy and beautiful description of different levels of heavenly kingdoms.

The Message of the Cross

A powerful awakening message for all the people who are spiritually asleep! In this book you will find the reason Jesus is the only Savior and the true love of God.

Hell

An earnest message to all mankind from God, who wishes not even one soul to fall into the depths of hell! You will discover the never-before-revealed account of the cruel reality of the Lower Grave and Hell.

My Life My Faith I & II

Dr. Jaerock Lee's autobiography provides the most fragrant spiritual aroma for the readers, through his life extracted from the love of God blossomed in midst of the dark waves, cold yoke and the deepest despair.

The Measure of Faith

What kind of a dwelling place, crown and reward are prepared for you in heaven? This book provides with wisdom and guidance for you to measure your faith and cultivate the best and most mature faith.

www.ingramcontent.com/pod-product-compliance
Lightning Source LLC
Chambersburg PA
CBHW020238130626
46549CB00005B/1945